FICTION

Contents

PAGE
64

PAGE
144

PAGE
158

FEATURES

FANCY THAT!

TEATIME TREATS

BRAIN BOOSTERS

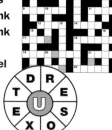

Secrets In The Smiles

Marriage, family and career success are among the many things that make our favourite celebrities happy

GEORGE CLOONEY

"I thought I knew what happiness was. I have a great career, many friends and people being nice to me for years. Then I got married to Amal and I discovered the real meaning of happiness. Having someone like her to share everything with is just fantastic. I have had this wonderful cake of life for so long but now I have the cream on top. Marriage to the right person is great, a real recipe for true happiness."

DUCHESS OF CAMBRIDGE

Kate, our favourite royal, is well-known for her ready smile and easy way with people, making them feel at ease. It was her smile and personality which first attracted William to her in St Andrews all those years ago. Since then she has travelled the world, engaging young and old alike, while at home she is patron of many charities. And of course, the growing Royal family is a source of joy and interest to us all!

AMANDA HOLDEN

"I think I am a happy person by nature but nothing really makes me as happy as when I am with my family, just being together, chatting and laughing. Christmas is a good time for that but it is not the only time. I try to have as much family time as possible – Christmas every weekend, if I can. Someone once said that you should like your work but love your family. I guess that's me exactly."

Continued overleaf

PAUL O'GRADY

"When you come home and your dog gives you a huge grin and has a tail wagging like mad, you can't help but be happy. It doesn't matter what sort of a day you have had, what worries you've got, your dog is always thrilled to see and greet you. At night your dog helps you relax because he will always curl up as close to you as possible. So, happiness is dog-shaped."

TESS DALY

"I am a positive person so I'm happy a lot of the time. I do get a buzz, though, when people stop me in the street and say how much they enjoy *Strictly*. You like to think you are doing a good job and you are enjoying yourself but really it is to do with other people enjoying the show. So when a stranger tells me they love it, that makes me feel happy that I am helping make them happy."

OLIVIA COLMAN

"I used to travel on buses and trains and people would look at me as if they were not quite sure if they knew me. Now they call me Olivia and ask about *Broadchurch* so I feel as if I'm recognised as an actress. That might sound conceited but everyone wants to be recognised for being good at what they do. I'm happy that people love *Broadchurch*."

LULU

"I am at my happiest when I see other people enjoying themselves. Sometimes that comes from an unexpected present, other times it's when 20,000 people have left their cares at the door and are having fun enjoying a concert. Happiness is infectious so when you are with people enjoying themselves, you cannot help but feel a warm glow."

Continued overleaf

JUDI DENCH

"I have been a happy sort of person all my life and I think I have a good sense of humour – quite wicked at times. I have also had my unhappy times, of course, and I think that one of the things I have learned is that you are happiest when you have someone special in your life. When you can share your life with another person you find yourself laughing more, feeling more relaxed, looking forward to things more. It's a great way to live."

CLAUDIA WINKLEMAN

"Happiness comes in many forms. *Strictly* winners are the happiest people on the planet when the results are announced, and why not? For me, happiness comes when you are well. Our experience when our daughter was accidentally burned taught me a lot about counting your blessings. Things could have been so much worse had it not been for the brilliant doctors and nurses at the hospital. Taking our daughter home was one of the happiest moments of my life."

Brain BOOSTERS

Codebreaker

Each letter of the alphabet has been replaced by a number. We've started it off – see if you can fill the grid! It should reveal which song was Annie's first UK number 1 with Eurythmics?

	9		5		10		14		10 **A**		21		20	
16	23	5	26	16	20	16	2		22 **N**	14	13	26	14	7
	16		6		16		6		22 **N**		26		25	
25	16	6	22	14	23		11	13	6 **I**	23	6	5	14	20
	17		4		14		5		14 **E**		18		17	
17	26	16	6	23						8	18	21	5	14
				22									14	
5	10	22	15	12						15	6	20	20	12
	3										22			
9	21	11	9	12						16	8	8	10	18
	10		21		10		10		10		6		9	
15	23	6	19	19	18	14	20		9	21	22	6	16	22
	6		19		16		21		16		6		10	
5	21	2	14	20	16		18	10	1	10	5	16	23	12
	24		23		8		5		14		12		20	

A B C D É F G H I/ J K L M Ń O P Q R S T U V W X Y Z

1	2	3	4	5	6 **I**	7	8	9	10 **A**	11	12	13
14 **E**	15	16	17	18	19	20	21	22 **N**	23	24	25	26

5	26	14 **E**	23	14 **E**		24	21	11	5		9	14 **E**	10 **A**	22 **N**	10 **A**	22 **N**	15	14 **E**	18

13	18	10 **A**	12	6	22 **N**	15		7	6	5	26		24	12	26	14 **E**	10 **A**	23	5

Lesley Downer

The Geisha And The American Millionaire

She was as icy as a snow maiden

The foreigner was very strange to Oyuki, yet there was something about his eyes, blue like the sky…

Oyuki had never danced for a foreigner before. As she floated graceful as a leaf on the wind, she gestured with her fan and her hands, weaving a story of lovers unable ever to be together, and thought of her own secret love, Shunsuké, the dashing young student. Yet she couldn't help but also be aware of the foreigner with

Continued overleaf

his brown hair and strange pale skin, watching her so intently. His name was Jee Yaw Jee, Mother had told her, and he was not just any foreigner. He was very wealthy. Oyuki tried to wrap her tongue around the syllables. It was the most outlandish name she'd ever heard.

As for Oyuki's name, it meant Honourable Snow. In Kyoto, city of beautiful geisha, she was the most beautiful and the most desired. Men admired her perfect oval face and porcelain complexion, her fine nose, delicate mouth and tapering almond eyes, and the exquisite grace of her dancing. But when they asked for more than just to see her dance, they were rewarded with a disdainful lift of her perfect eyebrows. According to reputation she was as icy and unattainable as a snow maiden, yet her aloofness only made them desire her all the more. People said that no-one

Shunsuké. He was witty, good-looking and very clever – everything that the rich merchants she had to entertain were not. He tied his hair back in a pony tail and wore traditional full pleated hakama trousers and a long jacket.

Whenever she could sneak away for a few hours from her duties at the geisha house she met him and gave him money to pay his way through university. One day, when he graduated, she knew he would be a statesman or a business leader and he would marry her and she would never need to dance for anyone again.

So she danced for her customers and kept her admirers at bay and whenever she had the chance secretly visited Shunsuké. For in the geisha world it was only permissible to sleep with men who paid. It was entirely against the geisha code to sleep with any man for nothing.

Then one day Mother, as Oyuki called the owner of the geisha house where she

Shunsuké was a brilliant, but poor, student – and Oyuki was smitten by him

could win her – and many had tried and failed to do so.

For Oyuki's heart secretly belonged to Shunsuké. Students were far too poor to attend geisha parties or spend the money required to woo a geisha, but the geisha loved their company and let them drink at the teahouses after hours for nothing or for just a few yen.

When the customers had been packed off home, the dashing students of Kyoto Imperial University would pile into the teahouses to chat, drink and carouse. It was then that Oyuki had met and been smitten by the most brilliant of all –

lived, had told her that a foreigner had come to town. He had heard of Oyuki's beauty, seen her dance at the annual cherry dances and had requested that she dance for him privately that night.

"Who knows," said Mother. "Maybe he will fall in love with you and marry you." But that was the last thing Oyuki wanted.

It was 1902 and in the ancient city of Kyoto, with its streets lined with temples and its tiny gardens hidden behind high walls, foreigners were a rarity. She occasionally passed one in the street but she had never been close to one, let alone had one visit her geisha house. People said they were hairy and didn't understand Japanese customs. Worst of all they ate meat, which made them smell different from Japanese, who ate only fish and vegetables. Oyuki wondered what this alien creature would be like and what on earth they would talk about.

As evening approached, Mother began to paint Oyuki's face ready for this first important meeting with this extraordinary new customer. She shaved her eyebrows and slathered white make up over her face, neck and shoulders, leaving a forked serpent's tongue of unpainted flesh stretching down from the nape of her neck, the most tantalising part of the body. The white make up made Oyuki look all the more mysterious. Then Mother brushed in "moths' wing eyebrows" like thumb prints high on her forehead, outlined her eyes in black and painted her lips in a rosebud pout of red. She helped her into her most lavish kimono, with a design of cherry blossom embroidered in gold and silver thread.

Oyuki leaned forward and gazed into the mirror. Her face glimmered magically in the candlelight. She wished Shunsuké could see her, that this painted beauty **Continued overleaf**

She wished he could see her

She dreamed of a new life

Continued from previous page
could be for him, not for a stranger.

Passers-by turned to watch as she stepped out onto the street of dark wooden houses with red lanterns glowing outside and made her way to the teahouse where she was to dance.

The foreigner was there, looking rather awkward, as if he was not used to sitting on the floor. She'd never seen such a creature before in her life. His hair was not glossy and black and smooth and straight like she was used to, but brown and bushy, parted to one side, and he had a moustache that hung to each side of his mouth, making him look a little like a spaniel. He was wearing clothes made of coarse woollen fibre – and he had no idea how to behave. He couldn't even speak her language.

She bowed and greeted him. Then as the musicians plucked their shamisens and the singers raised their voices in song, she slid one foot forward, then the other. She raised her arms, stretched out her hands and forgot everything in the movements of the dance.

The foreigner watched, entranced. When she had twirled her fan one last time and taken her last few graceful steps the music came to an end and she took her place on her knees beside him. He had brought with him a companion who spoke English and Japanese, and so they were able to exchange a few words. As she looked at him she suddenly noticed his eyes – not black or brown and narrow, like Japanese eyes, but large and blue, as blue as the sky. She gave a start. She'd never seen such eyes. They were full of honesty and also, she couldn't help noticing, of passion. She couldn't stop herself from glancing up at them.

As the foreigner sipped his sake he told her he was from a country called America. He wrote his name for her in strange, ungainly script: George – Jee Yaw Jee. At the end of the evening he gave her an enormous tip.

Soon George was coming to the teahouse every night and he always asked for Oyuki to dance for him. He even started trying to learn her language. He no longer brought his English-speaking companion. Instead he asked her to teach him words – rice, sake, dance… beautiful. She would make him repeat them again and again and laugh at his funny accent. One day he brought pictures of his family to show her. They looked at them together in the candlelight – his mother, his father, his brothers and sisters, the huge stone house where he lived in America, and scenes of America's wide roads and tall buildings. She noticed tears in his eyes and remembered that he was far from home. Foreigner though he was, he had the same tender feelings as she did.

To her surprise she found herself looking forward to seeing him in the evenings. She was getting used to his pale skin and brown hair and his eyes, blue as the sky. He no longer seemed strange to her. He was so gentle and kind and devoted, always bringing her gifts and paying her compliments.

Sometimes she wondered if her heart was softening towards him. But that couldn't be, she told herself. Her heart was

huge bustling city of Osaka.

There she flagged down a rickshaw and gave the rickshaw driver the address of the restaurant where Shunsuké was to meet her and they clattered off noisily along the cobbled streets. She was excited. She could hardly wait to see the young man whom she had loved so much and given up so much to help.

Now he had a job, surely today he would ask her to marry him? That was surely why he had told her to come to Osaka. But she also had some doubts. She'd grown fond of George. If she married Shunsuké that would be the end of her career as a geisha, the end of those fascinating evenings talking softly in simple words, dancing seductively, feeling his adoring blue eyes on her.

When she saw Shunsuké at the restaurant she hardly recognised him. He was as handsome as ever but he'd had his

She boarded the train for the bustling city of Osaka. It was a big adventure

reserved for Shunsuké.

In fact she hardly saw Shunsuké any more. He was working hard, preparing for his final exams. Then he graduated with first class honours. They had a celebratory meal together and he told her with great excitement that he had been offered a job with a bank in Osaka. He didn't need to say more. She knew he would want her to come and join him once he was settled.

For a while she didn't hear from him. Then one day he sent her a letter. She was to come to Osaka to see him. It was a big adventure. She set off, leaving the quiet streets of Kyoto which she'd never left before and boarded the train for the

long glossy hair cut short and he was wearing a dark western-style suit. There was something different about his face too, a cold look in his eyes. She felt as if she hardly knew him.

As the waitresses brought in the first courses of the meal, she looked at him in the glimmering light of the candles, waiting to hear the words, "Will you marry me?" This was what she'd worked for and hoped for all these years, yet now the moment had come she wasn't sure if it was what she really wanted. Suddenly she didn't know how she would answer.

He was staring at the assortment of **Continued overleaf**

Continued from previous page

tiny dishes on the table. Then he looked up, avoiding her eyes. "Thank you for all your help," he said, stumbling over the words. She looked at him with foreboding. Something was wrong. He was usually so confidant and debonair. "I really couldn't have got where I am without you." He hesitated, took a deep breath then scowled and looked straight at her. "But now I'm beginning a new phase of my life. It's not good for my career any longer to mix with geisha." He curled his lip as he said the word 'geisha' and she remembered that even though geisha were admired for their dancing and beauty they were also virtually outcastes, the lowest of the low. "I'm sorry. You've been very kind and I shall never forget it, but it's time to say goodbye. I shall repay the money you lent me as soon as I can."

She fled in tears from the restaurant. The next day when she went to dance for George she couldn't hide her sadness. In stumbling Japanese he asked her what was the matter. As she blurted out her story he listened gravely.

Finally he leaned towards her.

"All this time I've known there was something between us, some reason why you've always held back from me," he said. "But I've never given up on my hopes. I know I am foreign to you, I know my face is strange and my speech is strange too. I have only one thing to say to you. I've loved you from the moment I saw you. I want to make you my wife and take you back with me to America."

Shunsuké curled his lip as he said the word 'geisha' and his eyes were cold

It was time to say goodbye

For the first time she let him take her hand. The skin was different, not soft and silky like Japanese skin but firmer, more manly. She began to see that this man too had a place in her heart and that she could be happy with him.

So it was that Oyuki of Kyoto married George Morgan, of the Pierpont Morgan banking dynasty, and went to live with him in New York. There *she* was the foreigner. His family wouldn't accept this Japanese woman who spoke little English and who, so the story went, had been a geisha, which as far as Americans knew was tantamount to being a prostitute.

So George and Oyuki settled in Paris and it was only many years later, after George had died, that Oyuki finally returned to Kyoto.

Lesley Downer

The bestselling author's passion for Japan comes through in her writing...

Please tell us your inspiration for your writing?

I've been bewitched by Japan's wonderful culture, lore, literature and history ever since I first went to live there thirty years ago. I was lucky enough to live among geisha which has been a wonderful inspiration for me.

Where did you find your knowledge of Japan's people and culture?

I've lived in Japan for 15 years out of the last 30 and when I'm not there I'm always immersed in books about Japan past and present. I also speak Japanese and, I suspect, sometimes dream in it.

What was your first novel?

The Last Concubine, set in the shogun's harem, where 3000 women lived and only one man could enter – the shogun. My novel is the tale of the shogun's last concubine, when the shogunate was crumbling and the harem was about to close its doors for ever.

Do you have a favourite novel which you like to read?

I adore *The Tale of Genji*, the world's first novel, written by a Japanese court lady in the eleventh century. It's the story of Prince Genji and his many adventures and love affairs and it is as fresh to read today as it must have been then.

Where do you work, Lesley, and does it inspire you?

In my study, just above my husband busy working downstairs on his own books. It's close to the heart of London, near the greenery of Hampstead Heath and completely silent – perfect!

Do you have a new book which we can look forward to?

I do indeed! It's called *The Woman Behind the Screens*. It's the fourth in my quartet of novels set in nineteenth century Japan and will be out early in 2016.

Teatime Treats

Enjoy these tasty, tempting delights, and look out
for more fabulous recipes in the pages ahead

Apple & Blueberry Tray Bake

Ingredients (Serves 12)

- ✦ **100g butter, softened**
- ✦ **100g caster sugar**
- ✦ **2 large eggs, beaten**
- ✦ **1tsp vanilla extract**
- ✦ **125g self-raising flour**
- ✦ **Pinch of salt**
- ✦ **2tbsp milk**
- ✦ **1 small apple**
- ✦ **75g blueberries**
- ✦ **75g nut granola, or muesli if
  you prefer**
- ✦ **2tbsp toasted flaked almonds**
- ✦ **Icing sugar, for sprinkling**

1 Preheat the oven to 180°C,
fan oven 160°C, Gas Mark 4.
Grease and line a 16x26cm or
23cm square tin with baking
paper.

2 Beat the butter and sugar
together until pale and creamy,
using a wooden spoon or hand-held
electric whisk. Gradually beat in the
eggs, then stir in the vanilla.

3 Sift in the flour and salt, folding in
gently with a large metal spoon.
Gently fold in the milk. Spoon into the tin
and level the surface.

4 Thinly slice the apple on top and
sprinkle with the blueberries and
granola or muesli. Bake in the centre of
the oven for 25-30min until risen and
golden. Cool completely.

5 Scatter the almonds over the surface
and serve, sprinkled with icing sugar.

Banana Pecan Muffins

Ingredients (Serves 8)

- ✦ 200g plain flour
- ✦ Pinch of salt
- ✦ 2tsp baking powder
- ✦ 100g light muscovado sugar
- ✦ 50g sultanas
- ✦ 25g pecans, chopped
- ✦ 1 large egg
- ✦ 1tsp vanilla extract
- ✦ 100ml milk
- ✦ 50g butter, melted
- ✦ 2 large ripe bananas, mashed
  For The Topping:
- ✦ 50g pecans
- ✦ 10g butter
- ✦ 20g caster sugar
- ✦ 150g low fat soft cheese
- ✦ 2tsp icing sugar
- ✦ Dried banana chips

1 Preheat the oven to 200°C, fan oven 180°C, Gas Mark 6. Put 8 paper muffin cases into a muffin tin.

2 Sift the flour, salt and baking powder into a large mixing bowl. Stir in the sugar, sultanas and pecans.

3 Beat together the egg, vanilla, milk and melted butter, then mix in the bananas. Add to the dry ingredients and stir until just combined. Avoid over-mixing. Spoon into the paper cases. Bake for 25-30min until risen and golden. Cool on a wire rack.

4 Heat the pecans, butter and sugar in a frying pan until the sugar caramelises. Cool. Mix together the soft cheese and icing sugar. Spread onto the muffins, then decorate with pecans and banana chips.

RECIPES AND FOOD STYLING: SUE ASHWORTH PHOTOGRAPHY: JONATHAN SHORT

Christmas With Carol

It seems Jo and her sister-in-law will never see eye to eye – but can they at least avoid coming to blows?

By Claire Buckle

I f Carol starts, you'll have to say something, Mark. She's your sister after all," Jo said, entering the hallway to find her husband kneeling, attempting to strap their struggling ten-month-old son Tyler into his buggy.

"Well if she does, you could always just try to ignore it," Mark replied calmly.

Jo rolled her eyes and shuddered. She couldn't help it, she was dreading the thought of Carol and her husband, George, arriving for Boxing Day lunch.

"If she complains that our turkey wasn't free range or that I've bought ready-made veg then I'll be the one saying something. She's always making barbed

Her jaw tightened. Mark was too soft. She hated being put on a guilt trip by her sister-in-law and wanted his support. It was all right for Carol, a lecturer in ecology at a prestigious university, and George, a CEO in the City with his fancy hybrid car. They just had themselves to look after, whereas she had the family and a part-time job to juggle.

"And if she says anything about your diesel van, I swear it'll be the last straw."

"Please, give it a rest, Jo."

"I can't help it. I just feel so… urghh!"

"Paige," Mark called up the stairs to their four-year-old. "Come and get your coat on, sweetie."

Jo was now in full flow. "And what about the present they bought Paige last

"It's just Carol's way, because she cares so much about the environment"

comments and I'm fed up of smiling sweetly, gritting my teeth."

"It'll be fine. Don't be so prickly," Mark said. Having managed, despite Tyler's protesting squawks and kicks, to fasten the clasp on the safety straps, he stood and kissed Jo's cheek.

year? Adopt an endangered dolphin or whale or whatever it was."

"It's just Carol's way – because she cares so much. Let's not row about it, eh?"

"All right, all right." Jo shrugged on her sheepskin jacket and jammed a woollen **Continued overleaf**

She'd try to grin and bear
the barbed comments

ILLUSTRATIONS: MANDY DIXON, THINKSTOCK, MASTERFILE

hat on her head. "I care too. I want elephants and whales and dolphins protected too. But I don't want our daughter to know the world isn't perfect. Not yet, at least. Not at four years old – and especially not at Christmas."

"I do understand, love," Mark said, putting his arms around her and pulling her in close.

She rested her head on his broad chest; the soft lambswool of his jumper and the familiar smell of his spicy cologne soothed her for a moment.

Mark continued, "But I'm with Carol on that. I think it is important children know about these things. Paige wasn't upset, was she? And the charity sent that little soft toy with the certificate."

"I suppose I shouldn't get so stressed," Jo mumbled on a drawn-out sigh.

Her husband held her chin gently between his thumb and finger, tilting her face upwards.

"That's my girl," he said, pressing his lips to hers before Paige's voice interrupted.

"I'm coming, Daddy. Can Snuggles come, Mummy? He needs a Christmas outfit too." She bumped down the stairs on her bottom, squashing the teddy close to her.

"Of course, sweetheart," Jo said, with a smile and helped Paige into her coat.

Mark opened the front door and pushed the buggy outside. Jo took Paige's hand and followed, looking up at the sky, bleak and grey to match her mood.

Pulling the door shut, Mark said, "We hardly see Carol and George these days, so let's try and get into the Christmas spirit. Peace and goodwill and all that."

Some hope, was the immediate thought that shot into Jo's head as the four of them left for the shops.

Jo fixed on a wide smile as Carol and George arrived. Paige raced into the hallway, her little hand grasping a bag of chocolate buttons.

"No sticky fingers on Aunty's dress," Jo warned, eyeing the delicate floral and, no doubt, vintage, creation revealed as Carol removed her coat. Jo was well aware that Carol's passion for recycling often extended to items of clothing.

Carol dismissed Jo's concern with a wave of her hand.

"Oh, don't worry about that," she said and kissed Paige's head as George handed over two bottles of wine.

"A floral and fruity Chilean Red and a nice crisp Italian White," he explained, bending down to give his niece a hug.

"Thanks," Jo said, glancing at the labels. Obviously these didn't come from the local supermarket – unlike the bottles she'd just put on the table.

"Come and see our tree," Paige said, grabbing her uncle's hand.

"Yes, go on through to the lounge," Jo added. She'd been especially pleased with the realistic-looking tree they'd splashed out on this year. She'd managed to find some bargain red and gold ornaments and with Paige helping, they'd had fun decorating it. There was that special moment when Mark lifted his daughter up to place the star at the very top.

"Oh, it's a fake," Carol remarked, taking a closer look. "I thought I could smell a real tree."

Jo had lit a scented candle earlier in the day and the soft fragrance of fresh pine filled the room.

"Good. Just the effect I was hoping for," she replied, choosing not to let the frown that crossed Carol's face annoy her. "Now, how about a drink?"

While Mark was asking who wanted what, Jo went into the kitchen to prepare the food.

"I'll go," Carol said unexpectedly. But Jo was adamant.

"No, no. He might dribble on you and besides, he probably needs changing."

She hurried out and was halfway up the stairs when the microwave pinged and she heard Carol open it. Jo grimaced. No doubt there'd be a cutting comment slipped in somewhere over lunch.

Put some music on would you, love?" Jo asked Mark, as they all sat down to dinner and she settled Tyler in the high chair. "Everyone, help yourselves."

"This looks jolly lovely, well done, Jo," George said, gazing at the festive fare

The tenseness of the moment was broken by a sudden cry from upstairs

"Let me help you out."

Jo looked across from the sink at Carol, standing in the doorway. Ridiculous that her heart should start thumping simply because a container of ready-prepared swede was in the microwave.

She gave a tight smile and wiped her hands. "No need, Carol. Go and relax."

"Ah, you had turkey again," Carol remarked, ignoring Jo's instructions and eyeing the meat, sliced and ready to serve. "With Mum and Dad away on the cruise, we just had a small poussin from an organic farm."

"Really," Jo said, keeping her voice neutral and taking a gulp of wine. "We had my parents here yesterday and for them, Christmas wouldn't be Christmas without a turkey."

The tenseness of the moment was broken by a cry from upstairs.

"Tyler's awake," Jo said, relieved.

spread across the dining table.

"Thanks, George," Jo replied. The warm glow of pride lasted until she saw the tight-lipped expression on Carol's face.

They started to eat and began chatting against a background of choirs and crooners singing carols and songs. The melody of When A Child Is Born drifted across the room.

"This is Mummy's favourite song." Paige beamed as she tucked into cold turkey and vegetables.

"Well, it would be, wouldn't it?" Carol said, under her breath, but loud enough for Jo to hear.

"What do you mean?" Jo demanded, glaring at her sister-in-law.

George put his hand over his wife's.

"Carol, don't…" But before he could finish she had stood up and hurried from the room.

Continued overleaf

"I'm sorry," he said, making to get up.

"No," Jo said. "You stay there, George. I'll go and talk to her."

She found Carol in the kitchen, staring out of the window at the rain.

"What on earth's the matter?" Jo asked.

Carol turned an angry, tearful face towards her.

"It's easy for you, isn't it? No nagging guilt or doubts about anything. I ask you – prepared swede!"

"What?" Jo spluttered. "You're upset over some swede?"

"Doesn't it bother you that it came in another container the planet can't digest? And your fake Christmas tree will eventually end up in landfill."

"Tyler's crawling and I don't want the needles," Jo explained, in a bemused tone.

Carol raised her arms and dropped them to her sides in an exasperated gesture.

"Yes, and now, when I'd given up hope, accepted that it was just not meant to be, it's actually happened and for the first time in my life, I don't know how I feel."

"Happened?"

"Can you please stop repeating what I say, Jo. We've had IVF three times over the past couple of years, without success. Then, on Christmas Eve I discover I'm pregnant, naturally, after coming to terms with never having children."

"Pregnant!" Jo gasped. "Sorry," she said quickly, realising she was echoing Carol's words again. All that treatment and anxiety, yet Carol had never confided in her or Mark. Jo's throat ached – but she managed to raise a smile.

"Congratulations, Carol – it's wonderful news. The best Christmas present ever."

"Is it, though? It's come at a cost, and not just financial. It's tested our relationship and I'm forty-two now. The planet's overpopulated as it is and I'm

"I've not wanted to buy any children's things, reminders of what I didn't have"

"And a child is born whenever you've decided you want one. You've never had any problems." Her eyes glistened with fresh tears. "You got pregnant straight away, with both of them. You made a point of telling us that."

It was true. Maybe they had been a bit smug and joked about Mark merely having to look at her and she was pregnant.

"No waiting and hoping. I've been so envious of you."

"Envious?"

Jo's eyes widened. Why would elegant, wealthy, confident Carol be jealous of her?

adding to the problem. I'd convinced myself I wasn't meant to have a child. That I was an example of someone living by their principles."

"That's plain nonsense," Jo said, firmly. "You stress far too much over everything. You need to relax more. In fact, we both do. You're going to have a baby, Carol. A precious baby."

Carol's face crumpled.

"I've just been so confused – and if I'm honest, a bit frightened."

Without hesitation, Jo put an arm around her. It seemed the most natural thing to do.

"Everything will be fine. You'll be well looked after. Loads of women have first babies later in life."

Carol's stiff shoulders relaxed a little.

"Thank you. You're being so kind. I'm sorry if I've been spiteful to you sometimes, but I can't seem to help myself. I've not wanted to buy toys or children's clothes – all reminders of what I didn't have."

Jo reached for the box of tissues on the side and handed a wad to Carol.

"Well, now we can go shopping together. I know I can be over-sensitive and mean and, I'm embarrassed to admit, I've been envious of you and everything you have. It's about time I was more conscious of the environment, too. It'll be my New Year's resolution."

Carol wiped her eyes and blinked.

"*Really?*" She sounded so incredulous that Jo laughed in spite of herself.

"Of course. I'll start with… collecting rainwater."

It was the first thing that popped into her head – even though the garden consisted mainly of a scrubby lawn, with most of the space taken up by a swing and climbing frame. Later, she'd ask Carol's advice on other, easier ways of becoming greener.

Mark poked his head around the door.

"What's going on out here? Your lunches will be stone col…" His voice tailed off. Jo realised what a strange sight it must be to him, his wife with her arm around her tear-stained but smiling sister.

"We'll explain in a minute, love, but we're OK," Jo said. She dropped her arm from Carol's shoulder. "Shall we finish lunch? Then Tyler and Paige can open your presents."

They followed Mark back to the dining room.

"Of course, we'll choose a traditional name for the baby," Carol said.

Mark jerked round, his expression a mixture of anticipation and delight.

"What baby? Don't tell me you're…?"

"Pregnant – yes."

Mark whooped and hugged his sister. With a smile playing on her lips, Carol explained, "I was just saying to Jo that George and I would choose a conventional name, not a made-up, modern one."

Unlike Mark, who shot her a worried glance, Jo realised that her sister-in-law was teasing. Her face split into a grin as she winked at Mark and linked arms with Carol.

"You know, Carol," she said with a laugh, "I couldn't imagine you doing anything else!"

THE AUTHOR SAYS… "A radio discussion between two scientists with opposing views on climate change inspired the story. I'm with Carol on recycling and real trees but always have a turkey!"

Quiz Night

For Chrissie, sitting in the bar with her makeshift team, there was more at stake than anyone realised…

By Sandra Ireland

C hrissie, you are a traitor." Jack's thin moustache twitched alarmingly at the edges.

"You asked for it!"

"I've had to substitute someone else for this evening!"

"Tough!"

They were nose to nose, and Chrissie had adopted her battle stance, hands on hips, chin jutting. Neither would blink, on principle, until Jack snorted, turned on his heel and flounced away.

Chrissie smirked. For a fishmonger he was such a drama queen! He turned back to her just before he sat down.

"You won't beat me, Chrissie. And remember, I'm watching you!" He made that covert two-fingers-to-the-eyes gesture like a marine on point.

Expectation rippled through the crowded lounge. Men hurried from the bar with foamy pints on round trays. Women eyed each other over cool Chardonnays.

Chrissie had chosen her table with care. It was equidistant between the bar and the karaoke stage, where the quiz master was riffling through a ream of question sheets.

More importantly, it was right next to Jack; a mere twist of her head allowed her to glare at him with all the venom she could muster. She cradled her gin and tonic with one hand, while the fingers of the other tapped an edgy rhythm on the table top.

Her two teammates eyed her with amusement. Chrissie wasn't convinced she'd picked a winning combination. Joan, sitting opposite, was a pensioner who didn't get out much, and when she did,

A twist of the head allowed her to glare at Jack with all the venom she could muster

As Chrissie headed back to her own seat, the sound of a throat being cleared rumbled over the microphone, followed by an authoritative tapping.

"Testing. One two. One two." A small cough. "Right ladies and gentlemen, please take your seats. We are about to begin this year's Grand Gala Pub Quiz."

she insisted on taking along the comforts of home: milky tea in a flask, sherbet lemons and her crochet. Harriet, seated to Chrissie's left, was quiet and nervy, and whispered in a voice so low only dogs could hear her.

First, of course, there were the usual **Continued overleaf**

Cod Fillets
£12.50

Tuna
£20.00 Kg

Continued from previous page
announcements. The raffle prizes had been donated by local businesses and the Grand Quiz Prize was £100 and a voucher for dinner for two at the best restaurant in town.

"Nice," remarked Joan. "But how are we going to split that four ways if we win?"

Chrissie looked at her crossly. Joan could answer any question on handicrafts. Even now she was crocheting a blanket, hands flying beneath the table – but would she be any good on sports, say? Or current affairs? Did Joan even read the newspaper?

"We'll all go out together, put money to it," Harriet replied. "It'd be nice, a girly night out."

"We're having a girly night out," Chrissie pointed out. She took a swig of her gin and tonic. She wasn't sure about Harriet, either. Soaps were Harriet's thing, so she might be alright on Entertainment.

Glancing at the fourth, empty chair, she was beginning to regret asking Maz too.

"So who is the other team member?" Harriet asked.

"Maz Cartright," Chrissie replied.

"Is she the young mouthy one from the supermarket?" Joan frowned as she double-crocheted energetically.

"The one with the piercings and the sooty makeup?" Harriet looked worried.

Chrissie didn't like her tone.

"She has a degree in philosophy," she pointed out. "She might be a Godsend."

"Let's hope He sends her a proper Christian name," Joan muttered.

"Look, this is the best I could do at short notice." Chrissie was feeling defensive and hot. Maybe it was the gin; maybe it was pent-up resentment. She pulled at the collar of her turtleneck.

Always she had been seated at Jack's table, his right-hand woman. Always. She felt as if her arm had been cut off. She was wounded, like a mad Grizzly, and determined to get even.

And to my right," the quiz master was intoning, "are our reigning champions, unbeaten in four years. Led by our favourite fishmonger, Jack Sullivan, known to all as Jack Sprat – it's the one and only Clam Busters!"

"Favourite? He's the *only* fishmonger in town!" shouted someone at the back.

"He's got a monopoly!" laughed another.

"Isn't that a protected species?" shouted a third.

Jack acknowledged the good-natured banter with a thin smile.

Maz arrived in a flurry of outside air, smelling of cigarette smoke and leather. She was carrying a motorcycle helmet under her arm. Chrissie looked pointedly at her watch.

"Did you come on a motorcycle?" Harriet whispered, shocked.

"No, my hair always looks like this," the girl quipped, flopping into the vacant chair with a great deal more noise than was necessary.

"I thought you'd arrived here through a hedge. Backwards," Joan deadpanned, crocheting steadily.

Maz scowled and smoothed back her hair. It was crow-black with fuschia pink highlights, a colour repeated on her cheeks and eyelids. Her lips, by contrast, were a ghastly beige.

"My boyfriend is picking me up on his Kawasaki," Maz sniffed, "so I hope this isn't going to take long. I'll have a Tequila on the rocks and a bag of salt and vinegar. I'm famished, come straight from work."

"Looking like that?" Joan picked up a dropped stitch without losing her rhythm, missing the younger woman's lethal glare.

"I'll have you know I was voted

There was a rather long pause.

"Why are we here, exactly?" Harriet asked eventually.

"Because of him! He's humiliated me!" Chrissie hissed.

Jack glanced up on cue and narrowed his eyes. He had an all-weather look about him, deep furrows round his eyes and ruddy cheeks, as if he spent his life hauling in the catch and not merely wrapping it in greaseproof.

"Is it true," said Maz, "that you've been engaged to him for twenty-one years?"

Chrissie thought of the precious solitaire, boxed for safety and nestling in her underwear drawer. It had been the happiest day of her life, the day Jack proposed. Life had seemed so full of possibility then, glistening like the skin on a rainbow trout.

"Really, Chrissie?" Harriet bit her thumb nail nervously. "Is it difficult, working in the fish shop now you've fallen out?"

"Is it true," said Maz, "that you've been engaged to him for twenty-one years?"

Employee of the Month in March and again in July!" she retorted.

"I heard you were Miss January, too," said Harriet innocently.

"That was a charity calendar!" Maz snapped. "Look, I didn't come here to be insulted." She started to get to her feet, but Chrissie grabbed her arm.

"Sit down, sit down. Let's not forget why we're here. We can't squabble among ourselves. That's just what he'd want!"

She darted a look at Jack, who was poring over The Times crossword. He liked to limber up his team before a big quiz with cryptic clues and Sudoku.

Joan made a "humph" sound.

"If you want my opinion –"

"I don't!" Chrissie snapped. "Leave the questions to the quiz master."

Everyone had an opinion. Only that morning her mother had told her yet again she was wasting her life, stuck behind the fish counter, waiting for Jack to exchange the solitaire for a plain gold band.

"It's not going to happen now," she'd declared. "Face it, Chrissie; you've missed the boat. You could have gone to college and got a nice office job. Instead you're nearly forty, working all hours for a man **Continued overleaf** that doesn't appreciate you, coming home stinking of fish. What kind of life is that?"

Her mother was remarkably sharp for a seventy nine-year old.

It had been so different years ago. Chrissie had started in the shop as a Saturday girl when she was sixteen. At first she'd hated it, and scrubbed herself with carbolic every night to get rid of the niff, but the place had grown on her.

Suddenly the pong and the chill slipped beneath her radar. She learned to tell her bream from her lemon sole, how to dress a crab and cook a lobster. Soon she was the fastest filleter in the region, and kept

mahogany hair and bright eyes. Now she couldn't escape seeing the strands of grey when she looked in the mirror and her gaze seemed flat somehow, as if the light behind it was at a low ebb.

Oh yes. It had been so different.

"And the name is…?"

The quiz master's voice pulled Chrissie back to the present. She jumped, and the ice cubes rattled in her glass.

"Sorry…what?"

"What's your team name, Chrissie?"

"Oh, it's –" She glanced around at the hopeful faces of her team mates. Drawing her shoulders back she declared with sudden confidence, "It's The Torpedoes. We're going to knock the Clam

Greg, the genius of a delivery man, was scratching his head with a pencil

her gleaming knife in a soft leather holster on her belt. The customers loved her recipe ideas for the Catch of the Day and sales began to soar. Even the crushed ice in the display counter had a certain mesmerising beauty in Chrissie's eyes.

She fell in love, too, with the fishmonger's nephew. Jack Sprat was a quiet lad back then, but with Chrissie's encouragement he was soon twinkling at the old ladies, tempting them with this or that, and throwing in scraps for their cats.

When the fishmonger died and left the shop to Jack, it seemed that they were set up for life.

Jack proposed to Chrissie on her eighteenth birthday. The staff put balloons in the window and a sign that read "Congratulations to Jack Sprat and his Catch of the Day!"

She'd been young and bonny then, with

Busters right out of the water!"

Maz whooped and raised her palm for Chrissie to slap. Suddenly the game was on.

The questions came thick and fast, and Harriet jotted them down furiously on the score sheet in her neat receptionist's hand.

"Which artist created the Lobster Telephone?" intoned the quiz master

"Ooh you should know that, Chrissie!" Harriet whispered.

"Lobsters don't have telephones, they –"

"Salvador Dali," Joan interrupted, barely audible. She was still crocheting.

"Really?"

"Big fan."

Harriet scribbled, the quiz master droned on. Thirty-nine questions in and Chrissie was beginning to wonder if she knew these women at all. Who would have guessed that Harriet had read all the Dick Francis novels twice, or that Joan

Go Girls

was an expert on cricket? Even Maz pulled a few surprises. She didn't really look the type of girl who could name five species of potato. "I do work in the fresh produce section," she snapped at Chrissie's raised eyebrows.

By the interval, the quiz master revealed that the Clam Busters and the Torpedoes were neck and neck, closely followed by Burning Ambition, a team from the fire station.

"We can do this! We can do this!" Chrissie glanced across to where Jack was giving his team a pep talk. Greg, the bearded genius of a delivery man was scratching his head with a pencil. They were definitely under pressure.

"So why is this such a grudge match?" Maz leaned back in her seat and sipped her third Tequila. "Come on, Chrissie. Spill the beans!"

"It was six months ago," Chrissie began softly. "It was the final of the inter-county pub quiz league. A big night." The women nodded in sympathy. "It was the usual Clam Busters team: me, Jack, Greg, the genius delivery man and Malcolm, the Saturday boy. We were in the lead when suddenly the quiz master threw a curve ball. 'What is the capital of Libya?' he says, just like that."

"That's easy," said Maz. "Tripoli."

"Yes, Tripoli," Harriet and Joan agreed.

"Oh yes, that's easy to say now, but then, in the heat of the moment… Oh, the pressure –" Chrissie's voice tailed off.

Harriet squeezed her arm. Slowly she continued.

"I knew it was Tripoli. We all knew, but we just couldn't think of it. So I wrote down Tehran."

There was a collective gasp.

"That's Iran."

"Yes, I know," Chrissie replied irritably. "The point is I wrote down Tehran and it cost us the quiz. We lost by one point."

"But none of the other knew the answer either," Joan pointed out, wool flying through her fingers.

"But geography was my thing," Chrissie said. "I was supposed to bone up on it and I didn't study hard enough. I let the team down. Jack took it very badly. He refused to speak to me for a week, and told all the customers I was losing my edge."

"What?" Maz gave a snort of amazement. "You let him get away with that? And anyway, who takes this stuff so seriously?"

"Well, Jack does," Chrissie said. "It's his thing."

"Is it your thing?"

"Um. Yes, I think so."

"You think so? Chrissie –" Maz leaned forward. "I always thought you were a strong, confident woman. I really admired you. Now, I don't think I know you as well as I thought I did."

Chrissie's mouth opened and closed, a bit like a cod that had just been landed on a strange shore.
Continued overleaf

www.myweekly.co.uk **33**

"Sssh, here's Round Two," Harriet hissed urgently.

There was all to play for. The Torpedoes threw themselves into the fray, fielding questions on popular music, literature and sport with studied confidence. Eventually the papers were passed around and the marking began. As the quiz master gathered them in, they waited nervously for the result.

"I think you're bonkers, Chrissie," Maz declared.

"I beg your pardon?"

"Why are you still there? At the fish shop? With Jack? There's an opening at the supermarket. I can get you an interview. Tell him to get stuffed."

There was a spattering of applause. Chrissie sat frozen in her seat. Jack rose to shake hands with the quiz master and collect his winnings. Beaming, he grabbed the microphone.

"As you know, we have a slightly different line up this time." He glanced at his team. Greg nodded gravely. "There have been harsh words between us, but I want Chrissie to know Jack Sprat never holds a grudge. Not for longer than six months, anyway!" There was a burst of laughter and Jack looked at Chrissie.

"Chrissie, I'm going to take you out to dinner with this gift voucher!" He held it aloft as the other teams clapped. "And who knows, I may just pose a little

"Jack Sprat never holds a grudge. Not for longer than six months, anyway..."

"But I love the fish shop," Chrissie breathed. She'd never really thought about it before. She loved the neat rows of gleaming fish, the glossy tiles, the satisfied customers.

"But do you love Jack?"

Chrissie didn't answer. The quiz master tapped his microphone again.

"We have a winner but only by a tight margin. In third place; Burning Ambition. In second place –"

The silence was deafening. Someone coughed. Chrissie's nails dug into her palms.

"In second place, it's the Torpedoes! So our winners are… the Clam Busters!"

question of my own on the night!"

As the room burst into spontaneous applause, Maz kicked Chrissie's shin.

"See that job I told you about? It's on the fish counter. State of the art. And it's a management position."

Chrissie's face had been frozen. Now her eyes flickered.

"Get me the interview," she hissed. Rising to her feet, she took the voucher from Jack's hand. He was still grinning when she tore it into tiny pieces and flung it in the air like confetti.

"There's your answer, Jack Sprat," she said, and walked away.

THE AUTHOR SAYS… "I penned *Quiz Night* after my first foray into the pub quiz scene. I was fascinated by how some serious contenders limber up their brain cells with 'training' beforehand!"

FANCY THAT!

Fascinating facts about **Japan!**

✦ The Japanese name for Japan is Nippon, which means "sun origin".

✦ Geisha means "person of the arts" and the first geisha were actually men.

✦ There are 1500 earthquakes a year on average in Japan – sometimes many more!

✦ Japan has cafés where people can go to play with puppies and kittens.

✦ Japan has 67 flavours of Fanta, including Hip Hop and Genius Energy.

✦ Sleeping on the subway is acceptable as it's a sign of exhaustion from overwork!

✦ There are four different writing systems: Kanji, Romaji, Hiragana and Katakana.

✦ In Japanese schools the students clean the classrooms, staff rooms and cafeteria at the end of the school day.

In a Sumo training stable, junior rikishi Sumo wrestlers must wash and bathe senior sumo wrestlers – including the hard to reach places!

武士道

✦ Slippers only indoors – and when you use the bathroom in someone's home you change into other slippers so you don't contaminate the rest of the house.

✦ Noh, a type of Japanese theatre, can have performances up to eight hours long!

✦ The unemployment rate is less than 4% and the literacy rate is almost 100%.

✦ In Japanese, karaoke means "empty orchestra".

✦ Nestlé has sold more than 200 flavours of Kit Kat to Japan – including soy sauce and green tea.

✦ It is considered inappropriate to blow your nose in public – Japanese people sit and sniff!

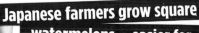
Japanese farmers grow square watermelons – easier for storage and transport

Little Brown Suitcase

Thrust together by the war, neither Charlie nor his Auntie Jean were prepared for this...

By Barbara Featherstone

The jangle of the phone startles me. It's late, and dark outside my small cottage, and I'm not expecting a call. I hurry down from the attic, my heart thudding with premonition.

"You will do it, won't you, Jean? I have no-one else to turn to. You do understand?" My brother's voice, tense with worry and fatigue, comes faintly down the crackling line.

And I tell him "yes" because there is nothing else I can say. I clutch the phone uselessly, long after the call is ended; my stomach sick with fear. Of all the favours David could have begged...

David will be so anxious. His words echo with my footsteps down the cobbled street. *You will do it, won't you, Jean? You do understand...*

All I understand is that this is one of the hardest things in my life I have been asked to do.

The train from London is already steaming out as I reach the station. Gritted smoke envelops the two figures – the man lean and tall; the small boy unwilling, hanging back – as they cross the bridge and clatter down the steps towards me.

My brother's kiss is brief.

"I'm so sorry, Jean. I know how

"You will do it, Jean? I have no-one else to turn to. You do understand?"

I don't go upstairs to bed. I lie here on the sofa, in the sitting room. It is almost dawn before I sleep, waking muzzily to the clank of milk bottles, and the postman's rap. And now I'm late. It's unforgivable and I'm breathless with the rush as I hurry down the village High Street to the train station.

difficult this is for you. But it all happened so fast. I have to do the best I can, for Cassie and for Charlie – for us all."

He sighs. "Nothing is the same any more. Our lives have changed. All we can do is to hope, and pray for peace again."

Then, suddenly, we are hugging each **Continued overleaf**

His blazer looked slightly too big for him

Continued from previous page
other, fiercely, with a shared grief and helplessness at the cruelty of war.

Up the line, a distant rumbling signals the approach of another train. David frowns. This is his train, but it's coming too fast, eating up the precious moments we have together.

My brother glances at me anxiously and then back at his young son. I try to smile, the promise between us unspoken.

I turn to look at the child. He is sitting, rigid, near the edge of the platform. He has his back to us, his bottom welded to a small brown suitcase. In front of him, the train draws in, shuddering and hissing, ready to carry his father away from him, back to London.

"Charlie…?" Softly, I call the boy's name.

He doesn't answer. The hesitant sound of my voice hangs trembling in the air.

Charlie is wearing his school uniform. Short grey trousers skim the bony cabbage knobs of his knees. Over skinny wrists droop the sleeves of a grey flannel blazer a size too large.

Everything is drab. The boy's school uniform, the thin straggle of passengers, the pearl-grey wash of the morning. The only touch of colour is a spike of the child's red hair escaping his cap. A dark gleam of red like a newly fallen conker. The words and the memory entwine in my mind like bindweed.

I try to call Charlie's name again but now my voice is just a whisper.

The guard strides down the platform. The train doors are slammed shut. There's a noisy bustle of expectancy, an eagerness to be off. Only the sudden stiffening of the child's back expresses his defiance.

David's mouth brushes my hair. Then he's hurrying across the platform to say goodbye to his son. He bends to kiss the averted cheek. Then he straightens, glancing helplessly at me, his blue eyes shadowed. The back of one swift hand knuckles his eyes. It is the first time since childhood I have seen my brother cry.

The whistle blasts. The flag is raised. David's train pants tiredly out of the station; my brother's face a worried blur through the sooty grime of the carriage window as he strains to catch a last glimpse of us.

Charlie doesn't move. A cloud of white steam separates us. For one wild moment I think… But no, the cloud dissipates and the child is still there.

I move swiftly now and kneel in front of him. His face is ashen, his body skinny and rigid. For a moment I forget the pain; forget how long it is since I last comforted a child. I circle my arms about him, pressing my lips to his cold cheek.

"Charlie…?"

Suddenly, I understand. It was the noise of the train, not defiance. The juddering, snorting, deafening, crashing beast that was the bomb shattering his terraced London home; the bomb making the ambulance come to take his mother away.

We walk slowly out of the station and down the cobbled High Street. Charlie holds the suitcase. We must make a strange couple. A boy in school uniform, incongruous in war time; and a young woman with pink plaits and poppy painted cheeks, incongruous at any time.

For four days, Charlie doesn't speak. He wears his uniform to bed, complete with cap and blazer, though the cottage is warm and cosy. He doesn't take it off, not even to wash.

"You'll stink," I smile.

He looks away.

have the measles?"

We make ourselves comfy, on the sofa. I explain to Charlie that I work in theatre. I'm an actress. But the war has intervened.

When David's phone call came, I was up in the attic rehearsing a play to help pass the time. I was so agitated by the call that I forgot to remove the make-up and the pink wig.

I tell Charlie this in words he will understand. He nods seriously. Then he races upstairs and drags the little brown

His question takes me by surprise. "Why did you have pink plaits at the station?"

David phones.

"Jean? The lines have been down. I couldn't get through. Cassie's going to be all right! Three weeks in hospital, they say. But she's going to recover fully."

He's babbling but happy, just about coherent. "The house is gone, of course. I'll need time to sort things out." He asks for Charlie but the line goes dead.

I bend and stroke Charlie's cheek.

"Mummy's going to be fine. She needs a little rest in hospital. Then Daddy will come and take you home."

Charlie nods, his face moon-pale, the dark eyes luminous. I anticipate a rush of questions but he takes me by surprise.

"Why did you have pink plaits when you got me from the station? And those funny red spots on your face? Did you

suitcase from under his bed. He changes from the crumpled uniform into clean trousers, and the bright Fair Isle jumper Cassie has knitted for him. I swipe a damp flannel over his face and leave it at that. This evening he can soak in a warm tin bath in front of the fire, his blue striped pyjamas airing over the fireguard.

Up in the attic, I show Charlie my box of make-up, and the wicker chest containing my theatre costumes. I dress up for him, acting out stories he will know. I hold up a mask to my face, laughing, inviting Charlie to laugh, too.

Charlie shivers.

"I don't like it when you hide. You're not you any more."

I stare at him, my mind racing, trying
Continued overleaf

to make sense of his words. Is this what I have been doing these past years? Hiding? Acting out a role to mask my grief?

And now I see it clearly. Charlie has done for me what I have tried to do for him – put a difficult concept into words so simple a child can grasp the meaning.

We go downstairs for tea. Charlie scoffs hot buttered crumpets, starving hungry now that Daddy has telephoned and his small world is mended.

He's suddenly chatty, too.

"Was that your little boy?" He points to a photograph on the sideboard.

I swallow at the past tense.

Charlie clambers off his chair and pads over to the photograph. Head to one side, he studies it intently. Butter trickles down his chin.

"Your little boy's got red hair like me."

A dark gleam of red like a newly fallen conker.

He flicks me a glance. "Sometimes,

boys at school call me 'ginger knob'."

He sleeves his nose and I say, "Don't do that, Charlie. Use your hankie."

Obedient, he takes his handkerchief from his pocket and makes a big show of blowing his nose.

I say, "Good boy, Charlie."

"Was your little boy called 'ginger knob', Auntie Jean?"

It's the first time he's said "Auntie Jean".

I tell him to sit at the table and finish his tea; my body trembling, my thoughts like flying shrapnel. While Charlie swigs a glass of milk and demolishes another crumpet, I begin the story.

"Louis was a very special little boy…"

But Charlie knows the words by heart.

"Louis was a good little boy. He was always happy and laughed a lot. He loved his Mummy and Daddy very much. That's you, isn't it, Auntie Jean? You're Louis' Mummy, aren't you? My Daddy said. And you love Louis very much, don't you?"

I hear my brother's voice, recounting the story. Charlie must have demanded it frequently. He has it word perfect, though his tenses are a bit rusty.

"But then Louis got a bad infection and he got ill and died. What's an infection, Auntie Jean? Daddy told me but I can't remember what he said."

He blinks up at me. "Daddy says it hurts you because Louis looks like me. Daddy says you don't want us to visit you any more. That's sad, isn't it? Where does it hurt? Does it hurt in your belly?"

He reaches for a chocolate biscuit. "Louis was only three, wasn't he?" He puffs out his chest. "I'm six. I'm a bigger boy than Louis, aren't I, Auntie Jean?"

Children are honest. They say what they think. Children tell us when they are hurt. They don't pretend, hiding feelings behind a mask.

Charlie licks chocolate from his biscuit then crunches around the edges.

"Will you miss me when my daddy comes to take me home? Will you get another little boy to look after?"

In my mind, I see my husband's face. I hear his gentle voice as he suggests we try for another baby. I think of his patience, his understanding. I think of all the times I claimed I wasn't ready…

A smear of chocolate is added to the butter. Charlie jabs a finger at the photograph next to Louis'. It's a photograph of my husband in his RAF uniform. He's smiling out at me.

"That's Louis' daddy, isn't it? He's gone to fight in the war. My daddy said the war is nearly over."

Somewhere, deep inside me, ice begins to melt. It's strange. It's not a cold sensation. It's a warm, tingly feeling…

Charlie snaffles another chocolate biscuit, his wary gaze on me. I forget to reprimand him. Pink-cheeked with success, he chomps at the biscuit. But he knows better than to chance a third.

"When Louis' daddy comes back from

He mulls this idea over. "He might get you a little girl, for a change," he adds

the war, will you ask him to get you another little boy?" He mulls this idea over, adding magnanimously, "He might get you a little girl, for a change. If you had a little girl, you could read her fairy stories. Girls like fairies. And you could dress her up in your pink wig and all those funny clothes. And you could paint pink spots on her face with those hairy brushes in your special box."

He sighs, replete with milk, crumpets and chocolate biscuits. "Little girls like dressing up. They like putting paint on

their faces." He looks at me accusingly. "Boys don't. And they hate fairies."

Charlie climbs down from his chair. He pads over to me and hugs his arms about my knees.

"Are you pleased with me, Auntie Jean? Was that a lovely idea about getting another little boy, or a little girl?"

I wipe chocolate and butter from Charlie's face. I scoop him up, press my lips to the spiky halo of his copper-red hair.

"You know something, Charlie? You are just full of lovely ideas!"

THE AUTHOR SAYS… "At an art exhibition one day, I was drawn to a painting of a 1940s wartime railway station. On the platform sat a small boy on a shabby brown suitcase."

Small Town Cinema

So many obstacles in the way of Ida realising her silver screen dream – not least her unreliable helper, Kurt!

By Camilla Kelly

October: When Harry Met Sally

Right. Let's talk about the film we're going to choose for our first cinema club. It's got to set the tone, keep people coming back every month –"

"I vote *The Godfather*."

"Don't you think… something more accessible? I've been doing some market research, and 70% of people said they'd most like to see a comedy –"

"*The Godfather*'s got funny parts."

"OK – something less violent, then. I don't know, I just think maybe all the killing and swearing might put off some of the older members of the community."

"I can't believe I'm stuck with you doing this. Seriously. You're the most obnoxious person I've ever met."

"You'll get used to me, Ida."

"No chance. You and me, Kurt Holland, we are not going to be friends."

November: The Truman Show

Ida was glad she only had to see Kurt twice a month: once when they decided which film they were going to show, and once on the night of the performance.

She still hadn't forgiven Janet for making her work with him. The Cinema Club was her idea, a way to bring the community together and raise money for the village hall.

"I can't believe I'm stuck with you doing this. You're an obnoxious person"

"If you're talking about Mrs Harris from the Post Office, *Alien* is her favourite film so I don't think she'll be put off."

"Not just Mrs Harris. This cinema club is supposed to appeal to the whole area."

"Who doesn't like *The Godfather*?"

"There are other films!"

"*The Godfather II*?"

Janet had insisted that Kurt's enthusiasm and film knowledge would be of great use to them.

"At the very least he can do the introductions. That would be good, huh?" She looked at Ida knowingly.

This was the problem of living in a **Continued overleaf**

place where everyone knew everyone else's business – they knew all their weak spots too – and since Janet wasn't just Kurt's aunt, but the mayor as well, Ida had to take her advice.

After all, it was Janet who would eventually rule on Ida's proposal to refurbish and reopen the old movie theatre.

So here she was, being pulverised by Kurt's "enthusiasm" as she did all the hard work. She'd set up the screen and was halfway through putting out the chairs. Kurt, meanwhile, was pointing a camera at her and filming every move.

"I'd rather you didn't," she said through gritted teeth.

"Just ignore me," he said, leaping onto a windowsill to get a more interesting angle on her face.

Ida scowled at him. "Can't you do something useful?"

"I am doing something useful. Years from now you'll be glad I documented the first few months of our enterprise. I might even make a short film of it."

She swore as she trapped her finger in a table hinge.

"Let me do that," he said, bounding towards her.

Gratefully she let him take it from her.

"Oh – wait." He handed her the camera. "Get a shot of me showing off my muscles."

December: It's a Wonderful Life

It was their most popular showing so far. Kurt arrived – late – to find the hall full.

"Where have you been?" she asked rather irritably.

He held up his camera. "I was editing some of the footage and I just lost track of time."

"Oh. I'm glad it was something important that kept you away when you promised you'd be here."

She hefted up a stack of three chairs, her tiny frame lost from sight beneath them. Kurt was impressed; this girl really was a marvel.

"Let me take those –"

"It's fine," she snapped. "I'm getting used to doing everything by myself. Really, Kurt, I don't know why you even bother to turn up."

Kurt watched hopelessly as she disappeared into the crowd of festive people. Smiling and greeting them, she looked like a completely different person to the scowling, stressed one he was so used to seeing.

I really am useless, he thought glumly. Ida was always saying she didn't need him and it was true – she'd be better off without him.

It would be better if I'd never been part of this, he thought, slipping quietly out of the hall.

No-one noticed him go. Probably no-one would even care.

January: Groundhog Day

Ida could barely speak to him. As they sat at a table across from one another in a café, she kept her gaze fixed on her peppermint tea.

"So…" Kurt said eventually. "We're decided on *Groundhog Day*, then?"

He looked miserable.

"Ida, if you'd rather I didn't… I mean, I can speak to Auntie Janet, tell her I want to give up. She won't give you a hard time; she'll think it's just me being my typical useless self."

Ida felt a pang of sympathy. She knew how hard Janet was to please.

"I never said you were useless," she said.

He didn't answer. She looked up and saw his raised eyebrow.

"Alright, I did, but I shouldn't have. It was a bit harsh…"

"It's because you care about the cinema club. I understand."

She glanced at him awkwardly. "You don't have to give it up on my account. Besides, I need you. We don't want a repeat of last month, do we?"

"I'm so sorry about that," he said, not for the first time. "I knew you hated public speaking but I had no idea it was so serious… At worst I thought you'd just announce the film and skip the after-show discussion. Anyway, I'm sure it wasn't as bad as you think it was."

She pushed her chair back and stood

February: The Artist

Kurt glanced up from his notes on that night's discussion to watch Ida setting up the popcorn machine she'd convinced someone to donate.

She'd never forgive him for leaving her alone at the Christmas cinema club.

At the time he'd genuinely believed his not being there would be a good thing, but now he saw he'd been horribly self-absorbed. From now on he'd try harder. He knew the value of the cinema club, he could see how everyone loved it. People stopped him in the street to suggest films.

For the first time in his life he felt proud of his work. He wanted to do his part in ensuring it carried on. Maybe Ida would start trusting him again.

Often, when he'd done everything he

He was mesmerised by the excitement on her face watching everyone arrive

up, gathering her jacket. He didn't know the panic she'd felt when she realised he wasn't there, the humiliation when she'd forced herself to stand up to welcome everyone, and with dozens of eyes on her could barely squeak out the title of the film before scuttling off.

Yet Kurt couldn't know that she was as disappointed in herself as she was in him. How was she ever going to attain the career she dreamed of if every time she was in front of more than two people, her tongue turned to salt and her brain to gloop?

"I'll see you next week at the showing," she said shortly.

She left Kurt staring after her, injured, and heard him say, "I wish I could do that whole day over again."

could do – printing the tickets, researching the film for interesting trivia he could use to entertain the audience – he'd put his energy into the film he was making.

Then he'd find himself watching the recordings of Ida, mesmerised by the excitement on her face when she saw everyone arrive for the first showing, or the way she lit up when the fanfare played before the movie.

He'd caught her on camera once when she thought she was alone. She'd been playing part of The Artist to make sure it was properly loaded. He caught her framed by the screen, her skin lit by its glow, the absorbed delight on her face. She was in the 1920s, as beautiful as any starlet. He couldn't stop looking at her.

Continued overleaf

March: Titanic

"Just relax, Ida. Nothing can possibly go wrong."

Ida gave Kurt a disbelieving look. "Apart from Janet thinking it's all a shambles, refusing me the lease on the old theatre, and deciding to stop funding the cinema club too, for good measure?"

"Why would she do that? We're getting bigger audiences every month."

Ida took a deep breath. This was Janet's first time attending the cinema club. It had to go smoothly.

Ten minutes before the performance the hall was crowded as usual, but the audience were on their best behaviour. Everyone knew that Janet was there and it had somehow got around that she'd be deciding on the fate of the cinema club.

Ida showed Janet to a reserved seat in the centre of the third row back – the best seat in the house.

"Lady Mayor, ladies and gentlemen," Kurt said, standing at the front of the room, "welcome to March's cinema club." He'd even brushed his hair out of its typical kitchen-mop style, Ida noticed, and she felt thankful towards him for making the effort.

"As usual we'll be holding an informal discussion after the performance for those of you who would like to stay, but for now let's get on with the film…"

Later she wondered whether the electrical supply had been over-burdened somehow by the addition of the popcorn machine, but she'd have to wait for the electrician's report to find out for sure. All she knew was, there was a pop and a spark, someone in the audience shrieked, and then there was the distinct smell of

burning just before the lights went out.

Immediately Fred Peters, the sullen caretaker, panicked and hit the fire alarm.

Grumbling, everyone mooched towards the fire exits, holding their hands over their ears.

Ida was mortified.

"Well," Janet said cheerfully, "at least I didn't get a numb bum having to sit through that awful film."

April: Cinema Paradiso

The projector wouldn't be fixed for weeks. April's cinema club was cancelled and they didn't know about May's. Health and Safety had decided the ancient hall needed complete re-wiring.

To take Ida's mind off things, Kurt invited her over to his place – and to his surprise, she came.

His was a small flat, untidy and over-stuffed with quirky furniture and fan memorabilia. She looked a little relieved when he led her through to the garden.

The garden was the one thing the flat had going for it. Not only was it a lovely, simple stretch of space, but it backed on to acres of meadows.

A couple of his friends were there,

arguing over a stack of DVDs and grilling veggie burgers on the barbecue.

"It's a mini impromptu cinema club," Kurt said shyly. "I hope you won't be too cold out here?"

Ida shook her head, looking at the extension lead running from the kitchen to the large flat-screen TV standing against the patio wall.

"We won't bother your neighbours?"

"I've chosen just the right film. It's one of my favourites."

They made themselves comfy. As the introduction to the film started to play Ida looked at Kurt in surprise.

"What?" he demanded. "Don't you like Italian films?"

"Well, to be honest, I was expecting *The Godfather.*"

He grinned. "Maybe another time."

The sound was kept low but thanks to the subtitles no-one missed anything. Kurt kept glancing at Ida, checking for her approval.

Eventually she leaned closer to him and whispered, "Thanks for inviting me,

people can come along and feel as if it really belongs to them."

She dragged her eyes away from the screen to meet his gaze. He wanted to say something, was desperate to find just the right response, but felt tongue-tied. After a moment's silence they both turned back to the film.

If only life came with subtitles, he thought. *Then maybe I wouldn't say the wrong thing so much.*

May: Field of Dreams

I t went pretty well," Ida said as she stacked the chairs after their first cinema club in the re-wired hall. "Considering…"

"It was great," Kurt enthused.

"I think that might be over-stating it."

"Not at all. Didn't you say you wanted a place people felt belonged to them? I'd say dozens of people turning up to watch an old film on a forty-inch widescreen TV because the projector's not fixed yet is a pretty good indication that they feel emotionally invested."

"I'd love a place like that, where people can feel as if it really belongs to them"

Kurt. I've wanted to see this film for absolutely ages."

"Reminds you why you love the cinema, doesn't it?"

"It makes me think of this place I saw in this small village in Ireland once. Someone was running a cinema out of their living room. There was a row of mismatched chairs and everyone brought their own cushions and snacks.

"I'd really love a place like that. Not quite so small, I mean, but a place where

Ida paused and looked at him, touched that he'd paid such close attention to her.

"Thanks, Kurt."

He turned away, but not before she saw him blush.

"I think you should be proud of what you achieved," he said. "And I have some news – Janet wants the cinema club to continue, mainly because she's sick of people hounding her in the street about it, but she wants you to work towards
Continued overleaf

moving it to a more suitable venue."

He reached into his pocket and pulled out a set of keys.

"The old theatre." He shook the keys on his finger so they tinkled like fairy notes. A wish being granted.

Ida put her hands over her mouth but still a little squeak of excitement escaped. She knew the place well: faded seats with broken springs; mouse-infested projection rooms; the plaster cracking on the mouldings; the damp, stale smell. There was so much work to be done to restore it.

It was going to be perfect.

June: The Fog

For weeks it was perfect weather for the workmen to get on with fixing the roof of the old theatre, and for hauling out the torn seating and broken equipment. Kurt volunteered his help too and was amazed how quickly Ida seemed to be getting the place back in shape.

Then the spell of good weather broke

ago, he probably would have phoned to make his excuses, but not now. Now he'd rather be hit by lightning than let her down. And was he imagining it, or was she actually pleased to see him?

She helped him off with his coat, but when there was another clap of thunder she jumped, her grip tightening on his coat, practically choking him.

"Ida? Are you alright?"

"Of course. Absolutely."

She looked pale. "Not a big fan of storms," she admitted.

"Ah. No problem. The scary movie will soon take your mind off it."

Ida went to the doors and looked outside. It was fierce out there.

Glancing at her watch, she said, "Somehow I don't think anyone else will be coming."

"Can't really blame them. Why don't we put the film on anyway?" He hoped she couldn't tell how fast his heart was suddenly beating. "I mean, it's a great movie, it'd be a shame to waste it."

"No problem. The scary movie will soon take your mind off the thunderstorm"

and there was a deluge of rain.

Kurt arrived at the hall for the cinema club with his raincoat pulled high over his head. He'd been afraid to use an umbrella because he'd heard thunder claps, and sure enough, lightning now flashed through the gloom barely seconds before the thunder rumbled.

"Kurt! I didn't think you'd make it." Ida greeted him with a handful of paper towels to dry his hair.

It hurt to think she was still expecting him to let her down. Admittedly, a year

"You're kidding! On a night like this, just the two of us in this whole place?" She gripped his arm, her face lighting up. "It'll be fantastic. Can we turn the lights off and everything?"

Kurt grinned. "Whatever you like."

"Whoever screams first has to buy the other a drink."

The big, empty hall was dark and silent, and it felt as though it grew distinctly colder once the film started. It was the eeriest experience of Kurt's life.

They were barely ten minutes in when

Ida – who'd crept closer and closer to him – let out a shriek.

"Alright," she whispered, giggling, "drinks are on me."

He reached over and took her hand. She looked at it a moment, bemused. Then she gave him a soft smile, gripped his hand more tightly, and didn't let go for the rest of the film.

July: Singin' in the Rain

It was a beautiful light evening and Ida was doing her new favourite thing: shining up her new cinema. Piece by piece it was coming together.

A song she loved came on the portable radio and she began to sing along.

Earlier she'd had an argument with Kurt – as usual – over this month's film. Kurt was one of those people who thought musicals were weird because normal people suddenly burst into song.

"Really?" she challenged him teasingly. "Because I kind of feel sorry for people who don't feel the urge to burst into song once in a while."

She caught herself singing all the time. She was in such a good mood these days.

Even around Kurt. Sometimes, perplexingly, *especially* around Kurt.

Now, she did an enthusiastic – if ungainly – spin across the lobby, her cleaning cloth fluttering after her like Cyd Charisse's scarf. Once at the other side she realised someone had come in through the unlocked doors, and laughed breathlessly when she saw Kurt.

"I had a feeling you'd be here," he said. "Need a hand?"

"I need a dance partner," she said, grabbing him and completely ignoring the terror on his face.

"Oh. Er… I don't…"

Ida, taking his hand, forced him to pirouette her. Kurt caught her automatically, and then bent her back over his arm.

"Well," he said softly, smiling into Ida's surprised face as he held on to her, "maybe I did learn something from Gene Kelly after all."

August: The King's Speech

The cinema still needed work, but the lobby was spick and span, the popcorn maker was running, and the principal screening room was freshly fitted out, so they were going to host their first cinema club in its new venue. All the regulars had been invited a little earlier than usual and were grouped on the pavement awaiting the Grand Opening. Even Janet, who was beginning to get a bit narked at being kept waiting.

Inside, Ida was hiding in a bend in the staircase, and Kurt was wishing they stocked alcohol.

"How about imagining them all in their underwear?" he said.

Ida didn't smile. Her face was the same
Continued overleaf

shade of white as the notecards being crushed in her sweaty hand.

"Ida," he said gently, feeling horribly guilty all over again for what he'd done to her at Christmas, "you don't have to do this. I can do it for you."

She shook her head sharply.

"No. I can't expect you to carry on doing all the work."

"What are you talking about?"

"People don't just come for the film. They come for the discussion, the conversation, all those funny, interesting things you tell them – how do you do that? I'm so jealous, you know."

Kurt stared at her in amazement.

"I…" he began. "I mean, I was only trying to make myself useful to you."

"Well, you are," she said, finally giving him a small smile. "I couldn't do any of this without you."

she was still pale, she nodded decisively.

He opened the door for her. Taking a deep breath, she stepped outside.

The nerves rolled in waves from her towards the crowd and back again as they felt anxious on her behalf. She gave a quivering smile and steeled herself.

"Lady Mayor, ladies and gentlemen," she said, her voice clear and robust, "welcome to The Grand."

The rest was lost under applause.

September: Love Actually

Cinema Club regulars Holly and Steve were the first to arrive, stopping in the lobby to buy popcorn and point out to each other the posters hanging there. They walked up the stairs to the screening rooms, chatting about how good the place looked. Ida and Kurt had done a great job.

The second screen was open and showing a new release, but all the loyal

She inched closer. Even in the dark, she could tell that his ears were pink

He felt a warmth begin somewhere in the pit of his stomach and spread to every finger and toe.

"You don't need to," he said. "I'll always be here."

"Well, I'm pretty sure I'm still going to need you to do all that, so thank you. But I just really wanted to do this speech today, myself."

"If you want to make a speech, you will, because I've never met anyone as capable as you." Gently he pulled her towards the glass doors. "And if I know you, you've practically memorised your speech. So all you have to do is deliver it."

He gave her a searching look. Although

cinema clubbers peeled off to keep their date with Screen One, greeting each other as they arrived.

Mr Ewan and Mrs Harris entered the screening room and took a couple of seats behind Janet.

"Evening, Lady Mayor," Mrs Harris said, greeting her.

"Not in my professional capacity tonight," Janet answered cheerfully. "Just an aunt."

"Is this something to do with the surprise Kurt's being promising, then?"

Janet tapped her nose. "Sworn to secrecy, I'm afraid." She sighed. "Isn't it great how well Kurt and Ida are working together? That was my idea, you know."

Gradually the seats filled up. Kurt stepped to the front of the room, smiling at the impromptu applause.

"Some of you will have heard that there's an addition to this evening's programme," he said. "It's just a short film, so I hope it won't try your patience too much." He blushed as he said it and mumbled shyly, "It's just something I've been putting together."

The lights went down and the curtains lifted. Ida stood at the back of the room. She had no idea what to expect.

People cheered when they saw themselves on the big screen arriving at the hall for the earliest meetings. Ida cringed as she remembered some of her bad moods, expecting at any moment to see some horribly unflattering depiction of herself.

There were sequences of the audience laughing in unison at one of the comedies, then arguing in the discussion afterwards about what made it so funny. There were shots of people coming through the doors shaking raindrops off their umbrellas, or slipping off their sunglasses, or clapping their gloved hands together – every time complaining about the weather. It got a roar of laughter from the audience.

When her face came up on screen, Ida could only peer through her fingers. She'd been so horrible to Kurt at the beginning, she was steeling herself to accept anything he chose to show. Ida nagging, maybe. Ida stressing. Ida complaining

about the untidy state of the chairs.

What she saw, however, was unexpected. She saw a girl sweeping floors, making tea, taking coats. She saw someone working hard to make people comfortable. She saw a girl glowing in the light of the cinema screen.

The audience fell silent. Everyone was looking at her, some glancing, some openly staring, with knowing smiles. Her face was taking up an awful lot of screen time. It was kind of embarrassing. Yet it was something else, too.

She inched closer to Kurt. He seemed to be avoiding looking at her. Even in the dark, she could tell his ears were pink.

She came close beside him, bumped her shoulder against his, and laced her fingers through his fingers. His hand squeezed hers tightly before he turned to her, and even though everyone was watching – or maybe because they were – she kissed him.

There was a faint sigh throughout the movie theatre, as when an audience sees a satisfying ending, and Ida felt their gazes move back to the screen.

She'd been meaning to ask Kurt something for a while now, but had been too nervous, but she was beginning to feel more confident about his answer.

She made up her mind to ask him tonight. She was going to ask him if he'd be her partner in the business.

She couldn't think of anyone better to run the cinema with. And it was clear that they made a great team.

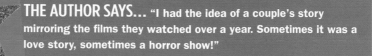

A Rub Of The Green

How could I go from being besotted with Matt to desperately avoiding him in the space of an hour?

By Lydia Jones

Y ou're quite sure about this?" Jess holds up Marigold-clad hands smothered in cream mixture.

"I am. I told you, he was practically salivating over that blonde in the movie."

"Yeah, but dyeing your hair is a bit drastic, isn't it? I mean, Matt asked you out when you were a brunette – and it's only been a month."

"I want him to look at me the way he looked at her."

"But she's a Hollywood actress. Besides,

We both giggle. A blob of cream drips onto the towel around my shoulders.

"Anyway, this isn't just for Matt. I'm not that sad – although I do really like him. It's for me – a spring makeover. I just fancy being blonde and glamorous for a change."

"OK." Jess begins to massage my scalp. "Prepare to be transformed."

Deformed, more like.

I gasp in horror at the mirror where my stubbornly brown hair is reflected back with an ethereal olive-toned glow.

"Jess – it's green!"

"Not this weekend. I'll text you." My stomach tenses with anxiety. "Promise"

I bet she looks completely ordinary without all that make-up on."

"Well – even if she does, so do I."

"No, you don't – I've seen. You're sure he wasn't just winding you up?"

"Mmm, maybe. I had just admitted to having a thing about Ross Kemp."

"Seriously?"

"Ever since I was glued to *EastEnders* as a kid."

"Amber, I'm so sorry. I did everything it said on the packet. Maybe we left it on too long. It'll wash out, won't it?"

"Hope so."

We scrabble about in the bin for the packaging, discarded in cavalier fashion earlier that evening.

"Twenty washes," I groan in horror. "Even if I do it every day, that's still nearly three weeks. I can't possibly let Matt see

me. Thank goodness I have to keep my hair covered at work. I never thought I'd be grateful for that stupid catering cap."

But I thought you couldn't wait to see this movie."

Bless him, he sounds gutted; I grip the phone, feeling guilty in my lie.

"I'm sorry, but Jess is having a bit of a crisis. I can't let her down."

Across the room, my flatmate grimaces.

"OK. Maybe I could swap the tickets for Friday?"

"Sorry." I twirl a still yucky-coloured hair tress round my finger. "Promised Mum I'd go home. I'll text you." My stomach tenses with anxiety. "Promise."

We have two more awkward conversations like this and then he says, **Continued overleaf**

ILLUSTRATIONS: SHUTTERSTOCK

Oops!

Continued from previous page

"Amber, is there something wrong?"

"'Course not." I squeak too fast.

"Only if you don't want to meet up…"

"I do. I do." My heart is thudding in my throat. *Believe me, oh, I do.*

"Well then –"

"I'm just busy this week, that's all," I finish lamely.

He thinks I don't want to see him," I tell Jess.

"Do you blame him? I've never heard so many weak excuses."

"Alright, genius – what would you do?"

"Meet him."

"And let him see me like this?"

"You could always tell him it's in honour of St Patrick's Day."

"Hilarious. I'm not Irish. I don't have any reason for looking like a leprechaun."

"Explain. You could say it's my fault if

"Well, then, you daft woman. Go."

"And I don't want him to think I'm going off him."

"So…"

Good to see you, Amber." He kisses me; I melt at the gorgeous scent of him. He sits, fingers stroking an unfamiliar woollen beanie hat. He looks more nervous than me.

"I missed you."

He's gazing right at me and he doesn't see; surely he must see. I offer up silent thanks for this empty table in the darkest of bistro corners.

"Thing is –" I run my hand through my freshly-washed hair: clean, fluffy but definitely still olive. "You're going to think this is daft."

"I thought you were blowing me out."

"What? No! It was my hair."

"Your hair? I thought it was my hair."

I offer up silent thanks for this empty table in the darkest of bistro corners

it makes you feel better. He'll probably laugh about it."

"Laugh at me, yeah. And worse, he'll think I did it because of what he said about blondes."

"You did."

"Jess!"

"OK, you didn't. Meet him."

"He did say he had a special reason to see me."

"What?" I say, puzzled.

In a slow, deliberate movement he removes the beanie hat to reveal the shortest Ross Kemp crew-cut I have ever seen.

He smiles; I start to giggle and lean forward into the candle light where my hair gives off its semi-luminous glow.

"I think you'd better get us both a drink while I explain."

THE AUTHOR SAYS… "This actually happened to me when I was experimenting with colour as a teenager but unfortunately it wasn't a wash-out dye and I had to cut my hair!"

FANCY THAT!

Fascinating facts about **Australia!**

The Tasmanian Devil has the jaw strength of a crocodile

✦ The world's oldest fossil was found in Australia. It's around 3.4 billion years old.

✦ **An Australian once tried to sell neighbouring New Zealand on eBay. Wonder what he asked for it?**

✦ The roof of Sydney Opera House weighs more than 160,000 tons. Its design was inspired by the segments of an orange!

✦ **Australia was the second country to allow women to vote, after New Zealand.**

✦ An Australian drinks an average of 96 litres of beer a year.

The Aborigine name for Ayers Rock is Yulara, which means weeping

✦ **The world cockroach racing championships are held annually in Brisbane.**

✦ No-one has died of a spider bite in Australia since 1979.

The Chinese "discovered" Australia at least 200 years before Europeans.

✦ The name Kylie derives from an Aboriginal hunting stick.

✦ Rod Laver is the only male Australian to win tennis's Grand Slam.

✦ **Emus cannot walk backwards.**

✦ **Australia's largest cattle station is almost the size of Belgium.**

✦ The country exports camels to Saudi Arabia.

✦ **Wombat poo is cube-shaped, to help it mark its territory.**

Before the arrival of humans, three-metre-tall kangaroos wandered Australia

Playing Cupid

The restaurant's Valentine Special evening meant that everyone's emotions were running higher than usual…

By Jan Snook

T he couple in the corner aren't having a good time," Jenny said quietly to Max, as she picked up two prawn cocktails for table three. "And prawn cocktail?" she asked in disbelief. "What is this, a Sixties revival night?"

"No, it's Valentine's night," her colleague pointed out reasonably, continuing to load a tray with drinks, "and prawn cocktail is pink. That's why we're serving fizzy pink plonk and strawberries. It's why the goat's cheese tartlet and the chocolate brownies are heart-shaped. It's why we're presenting all the ladies with a red rose. It's romantic, Jenny. Any other questions?"

He's probably making a complete hash of it. There's nothing we can do – except make sure they don't have to wait too long between courses," he said, looking meaningfully at her.

"OK, I'm going – but may I just remind you that I came in tonight as a special favour to you?" Jenny said, taking the sting out of her words with a smile. "And just go and top up their wine or something, will you?"

T he next time Jenny passed the bar, Max was assiduously polishing glasses.

"Where's she gone?" Jenny hissed, looking at the corner table, where Oliver was sitting alone. "Has she walked out? Is

"They're not happy. Just go and top up their wine or something, will you?"

"Yes. What are we going to do about the couple in the corner?"

Max looked in their direction.

"Oh him. Name's Oliver. Comes in a lot. I've never actually seen him with a girl before. Perhaps he's forgotten how to date.

it just the one goat's cheese tartlet then?"

"No-oh, she's just visiting the ladies' room. I hope."

"Table eleven is ready to order," Jenny said smartly, handing him her order pad, **Continued overleaf**

**It had to be a
perfect night**

Continued from previous page
and heading for the ladies' herself.

The girl from the corner table was standing at the mirror, dabbing at blotches of mascara on her cheeks. She looked up as Jenny walked in and burst into fresh tears.

"I look a total wreck. I can't go back in there – even if I wanted to," she sobbed.

Jenny took her arm.

"What's your name?" she asked gently.

"Lucy. And I wish I'd never agreed to this date. I've been wanting him to ask me out for ages, and then he did, and it was Valentine's Day, and I thought it was going to be really special. Now I find I'm just another girl to him. He seems to know all the waiters, and they're all laughing and joking with him, and asking after Moira, whoever she is. I just want to go home."

"Oh dear, I am sorry, but… Lucy, look, I only do occasional shifts here so I don't know who's a regular and who's not, but I do know one thing, I'm pretty sure none

would do anything in the world to be sitting opposite him having a romantic dinner. Still… at least she was seeing him this evening. Even if it was only because he was short-staffed.

Everything all right?" Max was asking as he topped up Oliver's wine glass.

"Oh yeah, great," Oliver said, rolling his eyes. "As you can see." He nodded at the empty chair facing him. "What am I supposed to do? I'm clearly doing something wrong, but I haven't a clue what."

Max eyed the single rose on the table. "Have you bought her flowers?"

Oliver groaned.

"No. I suppose I should have."

"Chocolates? Champagne?"

Oliver was shaking his head miserably. "I'm a bit out of practice with this sort of thing… and it's a bit late now."

"Well just tell her you love her."

At least she was seeing him tonight, even if only because he was short-staffed

of the waiters would talk about an ex-girlfriend in front of you."

"I shouldn't think she's an ex at all. Sounded as if she was current."

"So why is he here with you tonight? It's Valentine's Day and he invited you, not this Moira person. Come on, let's get you tidied up before the goat's cheese tartlet arrives."

Jenny looked at Lucy in the mirror as she dabbed at her eyes with a tissue, then looked at her own reflection. Would anyone be able to see what she was feeling? The way she'd been speaking to Max all evening, he'd never guess that she

"I should," Oliver said, sounding even more wretched. "I can't seem to find the right moment."

"Though why I should be giving advice I have no idea," Max said, suddenly serious. "I'm hopeless at the whole romantic bit." He looked up and saw Lucy making her way hesitantly towards them. "So what's her name?" Max asked urgently.

Well, they look a bit happier," Jenny murmured, glancing at the corner table. "Oh yes, look, he's holding her hand. That's a bit better."

"They'll be happier still if you stop

staring at them, and they can just have their desserts. Chef should have the brownies ready by now."

"But they ordered the strawberries…"

"Just collect their food, Jenny, before they get tired of waiting, there's a love." Max watched her tenderly as she headed for the kitchen.

"And believe me, I am very grateful that you came in tonight," he added, too late to be heard.

Jenny smiled as she placed the chocolate brownie – surrounded by strawberries – in front of Lucy.

Lucy looked at it, and then at Oliver. "Did you arrange this?" she asked, gazing at the icing on the brownie.

Oliver was suppressing his surprise well, Jenny thought, as he too gazed at the iced words:

Oliver ♥ Lucy

"Thank you, Oliver," Lucy was saying, still a little stiffly, as Jenny started to clear the table next to theirs. "That's really sweet of you. It's a lovely… gesture on Valentine's Day."

They were the last couple in the restaurant. Jenny could hear every word.

"It's more than a gesture," Oliver said, and Jenny's heart leapt. At last!

"Oh." Lucy spoke more quietly. "But what about the famous Moira?"

"Moira?" Oliver said, rather more

loudly. Then realisation dawned on his face, and he smiled. "Well, I'll be bringing her in here too, of course. Quite soon actually – on Mother's Day. That's what sons do for their mothers."

Jenny was still smiling when she reached the kitchen, where Max was getting a cup of coffee.

"Would you like one?" he asked her. "Your Lucy and Oliver are the only ones left out there, aren't they? You have time." He busied himself with the coffee machine.

"I'm really grateful you came in tonight," he said again. "I don't know how we'd have managed otherwise. I'm sure there's a disappointed man who wanted to wine and dine you, tonight of all nights." His voice was wistful.

"Well, actually," he added to the now gurgling coffee machine, "we could have managed without you. It's just that – I'm not much better than Oliver at saying these things – I wanted you here. With me. Tonight. On Valentines' Day."

"I wanted to be here," Jenny said softly.

Max turned round, still looking rather pink, just as Jenny handed him the second brownie the chef had iced that night:

Jenny ♥ Max

She could feel herself blushing, but it didn't matter. Max folded her into his arms, and by the time he'd stopped kissing her, the coffee was cold.

THE AUTHOR SAYS… "I once overheard a waitress say that the couple in the corner weren't happy. Soon after, they clearly were, which set me wondering, leading to this story…"

On The Escalator

Every nerve alert to the possibility of danger, Lorna finds herself worrying about fellow travellers too...

By Angela Pickering

Lorna was late. She tried to ring Peter on her mobile but her fingers fumbled at the buttons. The escalator clanked its way downwards and she stepped on, her legs trembling. She was afraid of escalators.

She knew she had to be brave as she had to use escalators, especially when travelling on the Underground. But the really high ones, like this current one, were a particular nightmare. She had to shut her eyes and hang on like grim death to the rubbery handrail.

She had always been nervous on the awful things; even as a child she used to think that the stairs would eat her up if she didn't jump off in time.

She thought that a lot of children must feel that way, judging by the looks she noticed on their little faces as they went up or down on the monsters. No doubt their mothers believed it was something they'd grow out of – but not if she was anything to go by, Lorna thought.

It all began that terrible and unforgettable day when she had allowed her mind to wander and she slipped. She'd been trying to ring Pete that day as well.

Her boots were new and her feet had seemed uncontrollable, as if they belonged to someone else. She should have known better than to travel wearing such uncomfortable footwear.

Her ankle had twisted and she'd fallen, bouncing from step to step, right to the bottom. She did remember, strangely, thinking that it was lucky there had been no-one else on the stairs at the time that she might have dragged with her on that awful journey to the bottom.

The rest of it was a blur, except for the pain in her ankle that lingered to remind her to be careful on the machinery.

Her grip on the handrail tightened and she opened her eyes to glance at the mobile phone in her free hand, wondering if she should try to ring Pete again. He would be worried about her if she didn't let him know she was on her way home.

She managed to smile at the little girl standing on the step below her. The child was a gorgeous angel with golden hair and the biggest blue eyes Lorna had ever seen.

"Hello," she mouthed at the child.

"Mummy, look at the pretty lady," the little one said, tugging at the hand of the woman who was holding on to her.

Continued overleaf

She should try to
phone Pete again

ILLUSTRATIONS: MANDY DIXON, SHUTTERSTOCK, THINKSTOCK

Continued from previous page

"Hush, Rosie," replied the woman. "We don't talk to strangers."

"But, Mummy —" the child began, but was hushed again.

Lorna smiled again, flattered by the girl's words, and made a shrugging motion as best she could without letting go of the handrail or her phone. Her shoulder bag swung and bumped against her side, and glancing down at it, she noticed that little Rosie was in danger. She leaned forward and spoke into the woman's ear.

"I know I may be over-reacting but your daughter's shoelaces are undone. It could be dangerous on the escalator."

Her mind filled with pictures of the little one falling from her mother's grasp — or worse, the laces disappearing into the

braved the escalator again. The woman glanced back as if she'd felt Lorna's breath on her hair; she smiled as their eyes met.

I t was strange," said the escalator woman to her husband later that evening once she'd tucked little Rosie into bed. "I don't know what made me look down at Rosie's feet." She shuddered. "If I hadn't — oh, Steve, just think what could have happened."

His kissed the top of her head where it lay against his shoulder.

"There is a rumour about that escalator, you know. They say it has a whatd'yamacallit, a guardian angel."

"You're joking. I've never heard that."

"Well, it's all rubbish, anyway," he said.

"I don't know. Something made me

She shuddered. "If I hadn't looked down – just think what could have happened"

machinery, pulling at the little feet.

The pulse in Lorna's throat was almost choking her. She edged closer to the woman behind her and tried again.

"Please," she implored. "I know it's none of my business, but Rosie isn't safe."

At last the woman glanced down.

"Oh my, darling," she exclaimed, "look at your shoes." She scooped the girl into her arms and arrived at the foot of the escalator carrying her.

Lorna breathed a sigh of relief. A nasty accident averted. She was glad she'd

check Rosie. And I thought I saw…"

She stopped, uncertain of what she thought she had seen.

"Mother's intuition, that's all it was."

Deep under the earth, at the escalator, Lorna stepped on to the moving stair. She knew she shouldn't have worn her new boots to travel. She glanced at the mobile phone in her hand.

I'm late, she thought. *I really should phone Pete. He'll be worrying.* But her fingers fumbled on the buttons and the escalator clanked its way downwards.

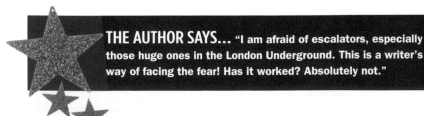

THE AUTHOR SAYS… "I am afraid of escalators, especially those huge ones in the London Underground. This is a writer's way of facing the fear! Has it worked? Absolutely not."

Brain BOOSTERS

Kriss Kross

Try to fit all the listed words back into the grid.

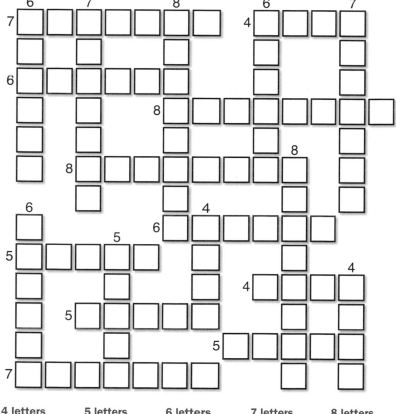

4 letters
Door
Epic
Road
Tsar

5 letters
Erica
Panic
Stamp
Tipsy

6 letters
Cohort
Demote
Hiatus
Sequel
Static

7 letters
Clamour
Clipper
Cockade
Rollmop

8 letters
Deerskin
Distress
Throttle
Unversed

Solutions on page 169

Greensleeves

It was such a kind thought of Rob's – he wasn't to know what memories that shade held for her...

By Veronica June

Moira turned the beautifully wrapped parcel over and over. It was bulky, squishy, and very naughty of Rob.

"I thought we agreed no presents," she chided, gently. That had been earlier in the year when the last fuel bill had shocked them both.

Rob had the little-boy-caught-out look. "I know, love, but it's your birthday."

It was hard to be angry with Rob when he looked at her so adoringly. Slowly she undid the parcel, one bit of sticky tape at a time, trying to guess the contents, drawing out the anticipation. If she was careful, they could re-use the wrapping paper.

She slid her hand inside, encountering the heating right down and all, I thought it would keep you warm."

Moira closed her eyes and lifted the cardi to her face. The wool caressed her cheek, soft, beguiling. It was beautifully knitted and ought to be a perfect present, but for the fact that it was, most emphatically, the worst colour green ever.

She tried it on, the sleeves flopping over her hands. Oh dear – it reached her knees and swamped her slender frame.

"It looked like your size when I bought it," said Rob, voice rich with dismay. He had the naughty-puppy look that always melted Moira's heart.

"Perhaps we could swap it for the next size down," said Moira brightly. Two sizes down, more like, and a different colour, with any luck. "Where's it from?"

He had the naughty-puppy look that always somehow melted her heart

something incredibly soft and warm. It felt like mohair and must have cost a fortune. Bad, bad Rob.

She quelled a surge of fiscal dismay, pulled her face into an incredulous smile, then opened up the package fully.

"Wow." She shook the cardigan out. "It is mohair. Wow." *Oh goodness me.*

"I know you've always wanted one, love, and now, what with us having to turn

How odd, there was no care label in it.

Rob stood up and put another log on the fire before turning and facing her. He was blushing, and not from the heat.

"Would you slap me if I confessed it's from a charity shop?"

Moira burst out laughing.

"Of course not. I think it was very sensible of you with the current financial **Continued overleaf**

situation, and truth be told, I'm relieved you didn't spend a fortune on it." She looked at him quizzically, suddenly remembering the prices some charity shops now demanded. "Or at least, I hope you didn't."

"It wasn't cheap-cheap but it wasn't a fortune. Less than a tenner, and I thought it would suit you."

"It's lovely." She'd have to wear it now – maybe she could unpick some of the length of the sleeve and re-knit the cuffs more tightly.

She'd hankered after a mohair jumper for years. It was very thoughtful of Rob, despite the no-presents promise. Now they were relying on the open fire for much of their heating, the central heating turned down low to save oil, she certainly needed something warm to snuggle in.

And looking on the bright side, at least it had lovely big pockets.

downs or jumble sale school uniform for her. And worse, Karen's mum used to work in the school office and was in charge of the second-hand school uniform cupboard, so Karen knew exactly who was wearing second-hand.

Moira and Karen had been best friends, but during that last year at junior school, Karen had grown nasty, turning all Moira's friends against her. Luckily they'd then gone to different secondary schools and never saw each other again.

The jeering rhyme started circling Moira's head, the memory provoked because the school uniform cardigans were exactly the same colour as this mohair knit. Moira sighed, pushed the cardi sleeves up, and went into the kitchen to help Rob with the dinner. Their daughter Alice and her husband John were coming over to celebrate her birthday.

"Is that Dad's present to you?"

Moira glanced round the shop. Maybe it was time to swallow her pride

L ater she caught a glance of herself in the mirror. Her heart froze momentarily, then galloped round her ribs. She remembered Karen Pickering from junior school, years ago, mocking.

Mousy Moira, muddle and mess, second-hand jumper, second-hand dress.
Karen had everything new – no hand-me-

whispered Alice as she passed Moira a coffee. "He's done it again, hasn't he?"

They'd eaten a lovely meal, and Moira had enjoyed every minute. The men were doing the washing-up, leaving Moira and her daughter to have a cosy chinwag.

Moira giggled.

"How did you guess? Only it's worse

than usual because it's from a charity shop so we can't return it."

"You might be able to take it back. Some charity shops are good like that."

"Maybe." Moira chewed her lip. "But it would be like spurning your father's gift."

"But Mum, it looks…" Alice fell silent.

"Ridiculous, yes, I know." Moira smiled ruefully.

"I wasn't going to say that. I was going to say 'on the generous side'."

Moira was showered and swaddled in cosy fleece pyjamas when Rob came to bed. He frowned and ran his finger down her forearm.

"Your skin's all sore from where the cardigan's got wet dangling in the washing-up. I'm useless at getting presents. I wish I hadn't got it now."

Moira stroked his cheek.

"It's fine, love. I'll take it back."

It was with some trepidation that Moira entered the charity shop with bag, cardigan, and the receipt Rob had sheepishly given her, and explained the problem to the shop assistant.

"I'm sorry," the woman said. "We only do exchanges, not refunds."

Moira cast a glance round the shop. Perhaps, given their current financial situation, it was time to swallow her pride and start browsing in shops like these. After all, it wasn't as if Karen Pickering would be there poking a scornful finger at her nowadays. And anyhow, she was forty-six and well beyond being bullied by a spiteful ex-friend.

"Moira? Is it you?"

Moira froze. It couldn't be.

"Karen?"

Yes; the name badge read *Karen*.

"I thought I recognised that voice. You haven't changed a bit."

Karen was smiling. Presumably she'd forgotten the nasty rhyme about second-hand clothes.

Moira gabbled out the story about the green cardigan, all the while wondering if **Continued overleaf**

Continued from previous page

she should suddenly remember an appointment and run away.

Karen laughed, a natural, joyful laugh, so unlike the spiteful scoffing that Moira remembered.

"Let's see what we can find, shall we? I've got a pretty good eye for what suits. I wanted to be a fashion designer when I was young. Do you remember...?"

Moira found herself reminiscing with Karen, catching up on nearly thirty years' news. If she didn't know it was Karen, she'd have found herself don't normally do this, but as it's you…"

It was fun, rummaging through the bags, exclaiming over garments.

Moira pulled out a pair of slacks from a bin liner. Under them was a thick, dark blue bundle of fluff. Just as Moira's fingers closed over it, Karen sat back on her heels.

"It's no good, I have to say something. We can't go on pretending just for politeness' sake."

Moira looked up guardedly, readying herself to flee.

Karen continued shakily, "I really

"Honestly, Moira, you always were such a mouse!" Karen jumped to her feet

liking this woman immensely. It seemed they had both lived in the town since leaving school, and they agreed it was astonishing that they'd never bumped into each other before.

On Karen's insistence she tried on several garments, but decided that although they were beautiful, they weren't very practical. They were the sort of thing that would lurk in her wardrobe, never to be worn but too good to discard, held onto just in case.

Most of Rob's gifts fell into that category, and she had a wardrobe full of them already. No; that cardigan had been a great idea, if only it had been the right size and colour.

"I wonder if we've got anything out in the back," mused Karen, "Come through, and see if there's anything you fancy. We

wasn't very nice to you in the last year of junior school, was I? I'm sorry. There were things going on at home which I wasn't allowed to talk about. Well, we didn't in those days, did we? Mum said you don't wash your dirty linen in public. So I didn't. And I saw you and your mum always smiling, always laughing together, and – well, I suppose I was jealous."

"You were jealous of *me?* But you had everything. New clothes, posh car. Anything you wanted you would have."

"Anything except a mum and dad who were nice to each other. I was so afraid they would separate, yet when they did, it was almost a relief, because the worst had happened. It was tough when Dad left, and it was I who ended up in cast-offs and jumble sale clothes.

"It was so embarrassing, but I made

out I was a sort of fashion guru and it was a lifestyle choice, not a necessity. I got really good at spotting potential and accessorising."

Moira thought about her own parents who had moved to the Lake District and still doted on each other. She'd been luckier than she ever knew; her parents always there when she needed them, a mum who taught her thrift and a dad who told her to always look on the bright side, just as she and Rob were always there for Alice and John.

She didn't know what to say, so she looked down at the garment clutched in her fingers. It was blue, shimmering as she pulled it from the bag. They both gasped.

"What is it?" asked Karen.

"Whatever it is, it's beautiful," said Moira, shaking it out.

It was a cardigan – mohair like the green one, but smaller and even softer, if that were possible.

"Wow, try it on," urged Karen.

If anything, it was on the slim side, but it wasn't tight. It wrapped her shoulders like a hug, warming her to her toes.

Karen looked her up and down.

"That looks lovely on you. Will that do as an exchange?"

"This is far nicer than the green one. It must be worth more than ten pounds, so best not." Moira look the cardigan off and

reached for a hanger, shoulders sagging.

"Honestly, Moira, you always were such a mouse! This one fits you, it's virtually the same as the one Rob bought. Of course you should take it." Karen jumped to her feet and put the cardigan in a bag before Moira could object. "Take it home, and if you really don't like it, bring it back and we'll swap it for something else. Though you seem to have tried on everything remotely suitable already."

Moira scurried out of the shop feeling slightly guilty, as if she'd cheated them somehow. On the door was a small sign asking for volunteers.

What a great idea. Maybe she could help out a couple of days a week, pay them back with work. It would do her good to get out and about, and it would be lovely to get to know the grown-up Karen – so much kinder than the poor, frightened, spiteful little girl from junior school days.

Rob pulled Moira into his arms and kissed her.

"Oh wow, that's amazing. You managed to exchange it, then? I didn't see that one in the shop. It's prettier than the one I gave you and I much prefer the blue colour."

Moira kissed him back. It was taking decades, but one day she'd have him trained in shopping for presents.

THE AUTHOR SAYS... "This story was inspired by my daughter's itchy school jumper, which she hated. She refused to wear it, even in the winter. Alas, it wasn't mohair."

Hidden Talent

Who knew what angry, frustrated young Ben's gift
would turn out to be? Certainly it was buried deep…

By Eirwen Fletcher

Some children live in their teacher's memory for ever; Ben Bates was one. The morning he came kicking and screaming into the reception class, dragged by his mother, I knew there was trouble ahead.

The peak of his baseball cap tipped over his left ear, a lock of brown hair covered one eye and his whole short, wiry body was a seething cauldron of anger.

"He's a bad 'un, miss – don't know what you'll do with 'im. All he wants to

picture. The figure was amateurish, but the patterned border he had created around it was bold and well-designed.

"That's very good. Is that your mum?"

"No, it's you." He spat the words out. He'd drawn a tall figure in a blue dress, with hair pulled back. "There's no silver pencil so I ain't coloured your hair."

I'd lived in the village for twelve years and knew most children by sight. I loved to help my reception teacher settle in the new intake, and get closer to them.

I felt sympathy for Ben; he didn't have much going for him. If he hadn't been the

Ben scowled at every child who came near him so he was still sitting alone

do is draw, won't learn 'is letters."

"We've had a few Bens in our time, Mrs Bates. He'll be fine," I assured her.

I took both his hands in mine.

"Ben… Ben, look at me." He wriggled, his shoulders heaving with intermittent sobs. "Your mum will be back soon."

When he'd calmed down I led him to a table with paper, crayons and pencils and suggested he might like to draw a picture.

"Can't draw," he yelled. "Don't want to."

Ben scowled at every child who came near him so he was still sitting on his own when I finally returned to him.

I looked with genuine surprise at his

youngest of four boys, with an absent father and a mother struggling to make ends meet, it might have been different.

"I've asked the council for a house," Mrs Bates had told me. "We've only got two bedrooms, so the boys do nothing but fight. Ben don't like it, 'e gets upset."

"Have the council put you on their exchange list?"

"Yeah, but we're no nearer getting one. There's going to be a new development over Marten way, but it ain't started yet."

Ben's home situation and his resistance to formal education didn't do him any

Continued overleaf

Continued from previous page

favours and he proved hard to help.

"Can't do it," was his eternal cry.

"You can try, Ben. Everyone has a talent," I told him, exasperated.

"Well, I ain't clever at nuffing," he'd say, his chin sticking out defiantly.

Ben's progress through the school had not been a happy experience for his long-suffering teachers so he'd spent a good deal of time in my study. He was there to work, and reading was a priority.

I was disturbed when he began to express aggression in his drawings, the patterns replaced by figures with knives.

"Who are those people, Ben?" I asked, pointing to the bodies on the ground.

Ben lowered his head and I could hear a snuffle amid the tears.

"The kids, me bruvvers, me mum… No-one likes me, they call me stupid."

"Ben, you are not stupid – and it's only

didn't find a solution to Ben's problems, he would move on to senior school with anger still bubbling below the surface. I feared what would become of him.

In January a solution appeared unexpectedly when Ben injured his knee badly in a football match. While his class were doing PE, I arranged for him to come to me for extra maths and English, always hoping to solve his problems.

As spring approached, I had noticed an unused area of garden. The authorities had agreed, and the area had been rotavated. I was ready with a last-ditch attempt to motivate Ben.

I bought a selection of child-friendly tools and showed them to him.

"Would you like to help me design a garden, Ben?" I asked.

He shrugged without enthusiasm.

"That's girls' work," he said, turning

I raised my eyebrows. "Your reading has improved considerably since yesterday"

your behaviour people don't like."

It was difficult not to put my arms around him; he was such a sad child.

After a while, things improved and I was hoping by the beginning of his final year that we'd turned a corner.

Then the inevitable happened. I arrived in his classroom just as he'd swept a display of pupils' ceramics to the floor.

"She called me an idiot," he roared, pointing at one of the girls.

I escorted him back to my study.

"I'm very disappointed in you, Ben."

"Sorry," he mumbled, sniffing.

What could I do for this child? If we

away. "Boys don't mess with flowers."

"My brother has a market garden and grows vegetables and flowers," I told him. "It needs a strong man to run a garden. First we'd have to clear all those small rocks and put them over there." I pointed to a corner of the garden. "Do you think you could help with that?"

"S'pose so." He shrugged.

When other boys arrived and started to carry rocks to the corner, he joined in reluctantly. What a strange child he was, unwilling to do anything himself but resenting others who enjoyed helping.

"How's your knee, Ben?" I asked the following week.

"Ooh, it's terrible, miss, couldn't play football." He rubbed the joint dramatically. "I could manage the garden, though."

He looked anxious, as if I was going to snatch something precious away from him.

"We'd better get on with the planning, then, hadn't we? I have these seeds and there are three flower beds. We need to find out how high the flowers will grow." I handed Ben a packet. "What are those?"

"Sunflowers, miss." He turned over the packet. "They grow to seventy cent…im…etres and you plant them in the spring."

I raised my eyebrows. "Your reading has improved since yesterday."

Ben lowered his eyes and picked up the other packets.

"Pop… pies, sow March to June, twenty centimetres apart. They grow to thirty centimetres high."

I was gratified; teaching Ben to read had often tested my patience.

"We'll put three packets of seeds in each of the three beds. How many do we need?"

"Nine," was the swift reply.

"Your arithmetic's improving."

"It's easy with real things," Ben said.

A bench had been set up outside where the potting could be done, and I watched, delighted, as Ben sorted out the seeds.

"Tall ones at the back, that's the sunflowers. Marigolds in the middle." He picked up the last packet. "Sweet al…ys…sum, five centimetres, sow in March. They can be in the front, can't they?"

Ben glowed when I asked him to show a small group how to plant the seeds.

"Come on," he commanded, waving to four girls who had joined the gardening group. "Over here, Susie."

Enthusiastically he explained where the tall, medium and short plants would go, showed them how to make a groove for the seeds with a rake, then handed out seeds and showed where to plant them.

"Well done, Ben, you're a good teacher," I said.

At long last he was looking happy. His confidence was blossoming and his behaviour showed signs that he was coming in to calmer waters.

Week by week the garden was eagerly inspected for signs of shoots, then buds. Ben offered to spend his lunchtimes and time after school weeding and watering.

One afternoon Susie shouted excitedly, "I've got a flower, Ben."

A sunflower had opened and spiky yellow petals had appeared. I joined them as Ben came over from weeding a bed.

"That's cool, Susie, that's so cool," he said, patting her arm.

More flowers appeared almost daily. When the first poppies appeared, Susie and her friend asked if they could pick some.

Continued overleaf

ILLUSTRATIONS: MANDY DIXON

Our garden was a huge success, much of it due to Ben's enthusiasm.

"Can I use those?" He pointed to the rocks in the corner. "I could do a rockery."

"If you think you can, go ahead," I said, "but most of your class are off on the venture holiday. You'll not have much help."

"I can do it meself, miss," he said, straightening his shoulders.

Had we really found his talent at last? As if fate was taking a hand, Mrs

miss. Go on then, give it to Miss Jones."

"You can have your tea in it," Ben said awkwardly, offering me a china mug. "Then you won't forget me."

"Oh, I definitely won't forget you, Ben."

Through the lock of hair falling over his face, I could see tears hovering and felt a lump in my throat. Ben was on his way at last – but I wouldn't see where he went.

"We'll have a garden at our new house, miss. Mum says she'll buy me some seeds."

"Goodbye, then, Ben." I felt quite

"I can do it all meself, miss," Ben told me, straightening his shoulders

Bates arrived one afternoon after school.

"We've been given a house on the new council estate in Marten, miss, so we'll be moving when the children break up."

"I'm glad, Mrs Bates. Flats aren't good for lads with lots of energy, are they?"

"Too true. But can I say something, miss? Ben's been a different lad since you let him do the garden. He spends all 'is time down the park reading the labels on the flowers and trees. He says you told him he'd got a talent."

"Oh, he has indeed, Mrs Bates."

The last day of term arrived and as usual a steady stream of children who were leaving came to say goodbye.

As I cleared my desk, Mrs Bates and Ben arrived. It was his last day, too.

"Ben wants to give you something,

choked as I held out my hand. "Good luck."

I used Ben's poppy-patterned mug every morning and often said a little prayer that life would give him a chance.

I'd dreaded this evening; after twenty-four years I was retiring from my beloved school. A ceremony and buffet had been arranged. On the stage with my colleagues, I surveyed a sea of faces.

A young man in the second row was smiling broadly, a lock of brown hair falling over one eye. Our eyes met and with a delighted smile I acknowledged him.

Ben pointed to the flower arrangement on the table in front of me. Removing the card, I read the printed words:

Ben Bates, Landscape Gardener

and added in untidy script, *Kindness and understanding are talents too. Thanks, Miss!*

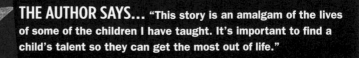

THE AUTHOR SAYS... "This story is an amalgam of the lives of some of the children I have taught. It's important to find a child's talent so they can get the most out of life."

FANCY THAT!

Fascinating facts about **Mexico!**

◆ The first printing press in North America was used in Mexico City in 1539.

◆ **Children receive their Christmas gifts on January 6,** when the country celebrates the arrival of the Three Wise Men.

◆ Pedro Lascurain was president of Mexico for just 15 minutes in 1913.

◆ **The Aztecs played a ritual ball game known** *astlachtli* **in which the losers were often sacrificed to the gods.**

◆ Mexicans have a national holiday known as Day of the Dead, when they honour their ancestors.

The *piñata* was actually introduced to Mexico by Spain, who pinched the idea from China.

◆ **An unusual Mayan weapon was a "hornet bomb" – an actual hornet's nest thrown at enemies during battle.**

◆ In Mexico, you can be fined for forgetting the words of the national anthem!

◆ Mexico and Luxembourg are the only two countries in the world spelled with the letter X.

◆ **The Aztecs believed the universe would come to an end and the sun would cease to move without human blood.**

◆ Mexicans drink more soft drinks per head than any other nation.

◆ **Founded in 1551 by Charles V of Spain, the National University of Mexico is the oldest in North America.**

The Chichen Itza Pyramid is one of the modern Seven Wonders of the World

Just The

How can Kate, stuck in a caravan in the rain with her three grumpy children, get this holiday back on track?

By Linda Priestley

I'm bored. This is the worst holiday ever." Craig sank his head into his sweatshirt like a tortoise and leaned back against the inadequate comfort of the caravan seat.

"We should've gone to Spain like when Daddy was alive," whined Rory.

Yes, well, maybe they should have done, but Kate couldn't afford it – never mind all the hassle of shepherding three

the Welsh countryside with her nature-loving parents.

She was mildly surprised that Rory, the youngest, could actually remember going to Spain with his dad, though it had been an annual ritual. They'd lost Gareth three years ago, when Rory was just five, and hadn't had a holiday since then.

"Shut up, stupid, you'll make Mummy cry." Becky, the eldest, off to secondary school next term, had a catch in her own voice. Craig retreated even further into his

She'd been trying to recapture her own childhood, not considering their needs

kids through the airport on her own. Renting a caravan in Wales had seemed like a brilliant idea, remembering her own wonderful holidays as a child, exploring

clothing, if that were possible.

"I'm just going outside to check the gas bottle," said Kate, and tried to smile.

"But it's raining," growled Craig.

Ticket

Becky nudged him and glared.

"It's easing off a bit," said Kate as she escaped through the door.

Outside the persistent rain had turned into a mizzle which obscured the stunning views. It dampened her face and clung to her clothes.

She pulled in a few shuddering breaths. Yes, she still missed Gareth, of course she did, but it wasn't just that. She missed masculine company and someone to share the pleasures and hard work of bringing up three children.

She yearned for manly arms enfolding her in a loving embrace. Holding down a full-time job as well as being both Mum and Dad to the children left her little time for herself, so it didn't look as though the situation would change any time soon.

Still, there was plenty of time for that; just now her main task was bringing up three contented and well-balanced children. Except, of course, they weren't contented today, were they?

The trouble was, she supposed, she had rose-tinted specs when it came to remembering her own childhood holidays. The caravan her parents rented had been far more basic, perched on a remote Welsh sheep farm, with ducks, hens and a couple of goats which the farmer's wife milked by hand.

Kate and her brother had run wild, making dens in the nearly woods, damming a small brook, climbing trees and reading books voraciously after supper, while her father and mother sat outside on camping chairs, contentedly watching the red kites – rare in those days, confined to a tiny corner in Wales.

She'd forced a nostalgic holiday on her own children, trying to recapture her childhood rather than considering their needs. Kids just didn't want to rough it nowadays. They wanted their internet and their electronic gadgetry. She should at least have booked a holiday cottage with **Continued overleaf**

ILLUSTRATIONS: MANDY DIXON, SHUTTERSTOCK, THINKSTOCK

wi-fi access. She should have braved the airport. She was a rotten mum to her kids, that's what.

Of course, the weather didn't help. Yesterday, to escape the rain, she'd bundled them all into the car and headed west, with no particular destination in mind, until they'd found themselves in Aberystwyth, which was proper seaside, and they'd had loads of fun, ice creams, chips, walking along the beach and the promenade, despite the rain.

Maybe they could go back there again, but she didn't fancy the drive – even though it wasn't that far, not really. She should have done more research, made wet weather plans – but in her childhood, the sun had shone every day.

"Muuuum, come in, you'll get wet," Becky called from a window. "I've made you a cup of tea."

standing on the platform waiting for the train home, telling herself that gnashing her teeth at her boss would just result in dentist's bills and not a nicer boss, when the carrier bag holding her shopping split, just as her train was entering the station.

She whimpered, staring in dismay at the milk, potatoes, bread and eggs heaped at her feet. The oranges scattered, while a maelstrom of disembarking passengers skirted round her as if she were a rock in a stream. In a panic, she grabbed the spuds, the milk, the eggs, but her hands were too full to pick up the errant oranges.

"Here," a masculine voice had said behind her. She'd looked round to see a good-looking man holding open a carrier bag. Her heart started pounding as her fingers met his and she stammered out some thanks. There was just enough time to shove her shopping in the bag and board the train.

Please don't fuss, she implored silently, an internal scream developing

Kate went inside and changed her cardigan for a dry one. Perhaps they could do a jigsaw puzzle – she'd packed a couple. Or maybe they could do some painting. Craig didn't enjoy that much but Rory liked it, and Becky was showing some real talent.

Would there be enough room on the diminutive caravan table? Kate pulled out the art materials, a couple of sketchbooks and some trays of watercolour, all tucked away neatly in a strong cream carrier bag.

Seeing the bag brought a wistful smile to her face. She'd acquired it a few weeks ago on a day like today, soggy, but windier, she remembered. She was

Kate almost wished the train had gone without her so she could talk to the man some more, but the childminder would have gone spare.

It was a good, strong bag, far too good to reuse as a bin liner, so she'd folded it up and put it away until she was packing for this holiday.

The recollection now filled her with an unfathomable yearning, a feeling of missed opportunity. The bag had a logo in green, and the word "Welshpool" caught her eye. She straightened the bag out.

Welshpool & Llanfair Light Railway. They'd driven through Welshpool on the way down. In fact, it was the nearest town

to them right now.
She pulled out the
map of the area. The
other place name on the
bag, "Llanfair", was even nearer,
though it seemed its full name was
Llanfair Caereinion, which sounded faintly
magical.

Fancy not realising before now. A
railway, eh? All three kids played with toy
trains and Rory was still besotted with
them, lying on his front and shunting them
round the living room carpet.

Perhaps they could go for a ride on a
train if it wasn't too expensive. If it turned
out to be too pricey, maybe they could
just watch.

"Let's go for a drive," she suggested,
not wanting to raise their hopes of a train
ride just in case.

"What – to the seaside again?" asked
Rory, a big smile spreading over his face.

"Not today."

His face fell, pouting, the very image
of his dad, causing her a poignant pang.
She hugged him and kissed his head.
Please don't fuss, she implored silently, an
internal scream developing.

"Not a boring walk," moaned Craig.

"We'll see." That scream was bubbling
perilously close to the surface.

"That means yes." Craig scowled.

Continued overleaf

"It means maybe," said Becky, and they all laughed because it was an old family joke.

When they pulled into Llanfair station car park, Rory squealed, "Are we going on a train?"

"I'm not making any promises," said Kate, looking towards the station buildings. It looked inviting. The urge to scream was replaced by an urge to sing.

"That means no," said Craig, though he was more cheerful now.

"It means, maybe," said Becky, and they all laughed again.

As Kate locked the car the kids raced up to the station. She followed more sedately, and they studied the timetable together.

It seemed the next train wasn't until turned into an engine, shunting round the shop. "Pshhhhhhh."

"Pardon me, but if you're going to ride the train today and tomorrow, you might as well become members of the railway," said a female voice behind them.

Kate turned to see a kindly-looking grey-haired lady wearing a railway cap.

"We do a Family Membership. It makes sense. It lasts a year, and members ride for nothing except on special trains."

She winked at the kids and handed Kate a leaflet.

"I'll think about it," said Kate as her purse cringed fearfully in the corner of her handbag. "But first, a cup of tea."

The lady smiled and disappeared into the ticket office while Kate bought a mug of tea and ice creams and sat down in the tiny tearoom with the kids.

A day rover ticket for all of them

"An otter," said Becky in wonder. "Wait 'til I update my Facebook status!"

one o'clock, so they had some time to kill. Kate was relieved that she didn't have to make any snap decisions about buying tickets. They could have a good look round, maybe buy an ice cream, have a cup of tea.

"I wish we'd got here earlier," moaned Becky. "Then we could have ridden up and down three times with a day rover ticket, had our money's worth. As it is, we'll only get two rides there and back."

"I haven't decided if we're going on it or not," said Kate, though it seemed the decision had been made for her.

"We can come again tomorrow," said Rory. "And the day after. I love trains. Choo-choo-choo. Whoo-ow-ooooo." He wasn't too badly priced, really, but if they were to come back tomorrow as well, then joining the railway made sense. The weather forecast for the week wasn't great, so a daily ride on the train would keep the kids dry and happy. All for the cost of a tank of petrol.

Kate went over to find the lady in the ticket office.

"If I'm a member, do I have to work on the railway?" she asked.

"No, but we're always happy to have volunteers," the lady replied.

"Can I drive the train?" asked Becky, eyes gleaming.

"When you're older, maybe." The lady smiled. "There are other jobs, though, like

all, we'll be *on* the train," retorted Craig.

They boarded and selected their seats. With a blast of the guard's whistle and a snort from the engine, the train drew away from the station. The scenery was beautiful rather than spectacular, and Kate was entranced.

There were wild flowers on the banks beside the railway, and the train was travelling slowly enough for her to enjoy them. The green countryside undulated around them, and rabbits and pheasants scattered in the fields as the train clanked past. The sheep dotted the fields like a sprinkling of marshmallows while birds soared overhead.

"An eagle, an eagle," yelled Rory, pointing wildly.

"A buzzard," corrected Kate. "But it looks huge because it's so close."

The train crossed the river Banwy. "What's that? Quick, look," cried Becky.

"An otter. I don't believe it. That was an otter," said Kate, tingling all over.

"I didn't see it," wailed Craig. "We have to come back now."

"An otter," said Becky in wonder, hugging herself with glee. "I've seen an otter. Wait 'til I update my Facebook status! Everyone will be well jealous."

The sound of the train on the tracks was oddly soothing, and Kate fell into something of a reverie. She'd loved Gareth dearly, but that was in the past now. She'd grown isolated and inward-looking with the effort of bringing up the kids while struggling with her own grief.

Still, they'd survived. Even so, there were times when she felt like an automaton, a robot mum, and not Kate at all. Maybe she needed to get out more,

Continued overleaf

station master, guard, helping in the tea rooms or the shop, working in the engine sheds… When you're older," she repeated hastily, because Craig looked as if he was about to demand to be allowed to get to work immediately.

"Well, OK then, can we join, please?"

Once the formalities were completed, the lady told them all about the railway. The kids were agog. Kate watched their happy faces and felt her shoulders loosen.

I must have been more stressed than I realised, she told herself.

The train came into the station with clouds of steam billowing around it, and they watched the engine being uncoupled and moved round to the front. All three children were boggle-eyed, and Rory was beside himself with delight.

"Cool," cooed Craig. "Cool." He took some photos. Lots of photos.

"It's just like *The Railway Children,*" said Becky. "Maybe we'll see an Old Gentleman waving from the train."

"I don't think that will happen. After

Continued from previous page
start being Kate again, and not just the kids' mum.

Thinking about it, the railway wasn't that far away – a two and a half hour drive. They could come up for the occasional weekend, do something they all enjoyed which didn't involve computers or electronics. It would be fun.

"I want to buy something from the shop," announced Rory when the train arrived at Welshpool.

"That money has been burning a hole in your pocket," chided Kate. "Don't spend it just for the sake of it."

"But I want to," said Rory, clutching a toy engine. They went to pay for it, and it had been entirely subconscious.

"Sorry to hear that." It was an automatic response. Perhaps he was sorry in a sympathetic way, but in another way, he seemed somewhat relieved.

When she told him they'd become members, he smiled. She explained about the carrier bag. His smile grew broader.

"I carried that bag in my pocket for years. And in a roundabout way, it brought you here. I'm glad – really glad."

"Mum, we need to get on the train because it's about to go back to Llanfair." Becky tugged at Kate's arm.

Kate flinched in alarm.

"We've got to go. But we're coming back on the later train."

"In a roundabout way, that bag brought you here. I'm glad – really glad"

Kate's heart lurched in her chest.

Was it? Could it be?

The man took Rory's money gravely before giving her a friendly smile, which froze, his eyes widening into a question.

"Do I…?"

"It is you, isn't it? The man with the carrier bag?"

"The lady on the platform. You looked as if you were having a horrible day."

"I was."

"And this is your family?"

"Yes, just us now, I lost my husband three years ago." She blushed at the implication of that remark, even though

"Good. I'll still be on duty here. Maybe we can talk some more then?"

Kate followed her children into the carriage. The man stood on the platform. She seemed to have a habit of jumping on trains in a hurry around him, she thought, and giggled. They waved as the train left.

"He's nice," said Rory, running his new engine along the seat.

"Yes, he is, rather, isn't he?" said Kate. Yes indeed. Nice, kind, gallant. Yes.

Becky caught her eye and grinned.

"This is the best holiday ever," declared Craig.

THE AUTHOR SAYS… "My husband is a volunteer on the Welshpool & Llanfair Light Railway. Tidying up, I came across one of their carrier bags containing my sketchbook and paints."

Brain BOOSTERS

Missing Link

The answer to each clue is a word which has a link with each of the three words listed. This word may come at the end (eg **HEAD** linked with **BEACH, BIG, HAMMER**), at the beginning (eg **BLACK** linked with **BEAUTY, BOARD** and **JACK**) or a mixture of the two (eg **STONE** linked with **HAIL, LIME** and **WALL**).

ACROSS

1. Cut, Ceiling, Fibre (5)
4. Luggage, Sticky, Warning (5)
7. Favourite, Hold, Stand (4)
8. By, Prone, Traffic (8)
9. Carrier, Person, Towns (6)
11. Early, Mat, Towel (4)
12. Black, Cage, Humming (4)
14. Hair, Hand, Pistol (4)
17. Bell, Circus, Peg (4)
18. Holy, Last, Marching (6)
19. Box, Mail, Rider (8)
21. Drum, Generation, Up (4)
22. Ceremony, George, Ribbon (5)
23. Angle, Down, Wing (5)

DOWN

1. Equatorial, Fowl, Pig (6)
2. Chair, Fire, Wrestling (3)
3. Fright, Landing, Struck (5)
4. Central, Horns, Inter (7)
5. Luck, Mouth, Timing (3)
6. Knee, Wave, Ways (6)
10. Blank, Match, Needle (5)
11. Colour, Date, Fold (5)
13. Camera, Recording, Watch (7)
15. Build, Happy, Rare (6)
16. Bone, Chimney, Stroke (6)
18. None, Wise, Worldly (5)
20. Bachelor, Key, Launch (3)
21. Business, Game, Wig (3)

Solutions on page 169

Dressing With Care

Everything is perfect, just like Sylvie herself. I've followed her instructions – but still I feel so troubled

By Tess Niland Kimber

I can't help it; I'm looking for Sylvie whenever the gate opens or a guest arrives. Over the sea of heads and around the corner of the conservatory where the security light shines into the snaking alley, I search for my old friend.

I think, *She'll be here soon, rushing and apologising as she sweeps into the garden on a cloud of Gucci perfume.*

Although it's August, the light's already fading and with the disappearing sun, the

Helium-filled balloons printed with silver 50s are tied to the dogwood tree branches which overhang the yellowing lawn. The atmosphere shouts "party" and, in the background, music plays over the sound system. It's Adele – Sylvie's favourite singer.

I bite my lip. I'm nervous…

The air's cooling but I'm trembling as if the mercury's tumbling towards freezing. I look up. Stars splatter the night sky like cosmic freckles.

"I want everyone to dress up, Carla," Sylvie had commanded months ago when

Helium balloons are tied to the dogwood branches that overhang the lawn

warmth evaporates. I shiver. If this was just a family barbecue I'd be wearing jeans and a fleece. But it's a special occasion tonight and I've dressed with care. More so than ever…

Coated by the aroma of the barbecue, we all stand in Tom and Sylvie's wide garden. Dancing along the wooden fence are a trail of coloured fairy lights.

this party was first suggested as a way to celebrate her milestone birthday. "Even you."

"Really?" I'd said, screwing up my nose. "It's a barbecue, Sylvie."

"Yes, and it'll be *my* barbecue so…"

"What you say, goes?"

"Right!" she'd smiled and, that time,

Continued overleaf

I love dressing up –
just not when I'm
going to see Sylvie

Continued from previous page

I'd laughed away my irritation. I loved dressing up – just not if I was going to be with Sylvie…

Tonight, though, I've done as she asked and dressed carefully. To any gate-crasher, it would appear I've gone way over the top. I'm wearing a long, silver dress – more red-carpet than garden-party. There's a rash of sequins over one shoulder with an identical pinch around the waist. Even my make-up's been applied as if I've developed OCD and before leaving home this evening, I'd practised my smile in front of the mirror.

"Happy birthday, Sylvie. You look great tonight…"

The words had sounded as hollow as a chocolate Easter egg.

last argument – a stupid tiff over her timekeeping when we met for lunch, all those weeks ago.

"Well, if that's how you feel…" she'd said, her eyes, blazing.

"It is – yes."

"Then…"

I watched her flounce out of the coffee shop as I sat still with as much dignity as I could muster, my face torched red with my already regretted comments.

After all these weeks of torment, I've put that stupid argument behind me. Knowing now that there are so many more important things in life than bickering about being late. Or where to eat lunch. Or any of the other silly reasons we've used over the years to argue.

"It's because Sylvie's a Leo, you see,

"So you came after all, Carla?" It's Tom, with shadows under his dark eyes

Oh, she'd look great, I knew she would. No matter how hard I tried, she always came first in our glamour stakes. No doubt, she'd wear the latest design, classy but sensual, robbing every man of his breath. How many times during our long friendship had I envied her effortless style?

Yes, she'd laugh and throw her arms out to indicate her surprise to see such a gathering of friends and family.

"And you all came for me?" she'd say, modesty part of her charm.

"Of course – we longed to see you again," I'd say, my platitudes as futile as a payday loan promise.

You see, I wasn't sure I could go tonight. Or even that I'd be welcome. All week I'd dithered, remembering our

love," my mum had once explained.

"A Leo? What do you mean?"

"Her star sign. You're Taurus. The two zodiac signs clash like red and yellow."

I'd shrugged but, surfing the internet later, I'd been intrigued enough to look it up. Mum was right. Leo – a fire sign – was incompatible with Taurus.

It was mad. We never argued over anything worth the effort. All the years I've known her, we've never squabbled over boyfriends or money or the children.

So despite those angry words, I've come to the party; I'm here now, standing with the other guests. There's Sylvie's boss from the estate agency, and, over on the

decking, is our dusty old geography teacher. We're all oohing and aahing over the firework display and I think it's not a bad 50th birthday party. It almost has the right ingredients for a great night. Barbecue, fireworks, plenty of family and friends – dressed up to the high eights if not the nines.

I look for Sylvie again. If only she'd arrive, wearing some drop-dead-gorgeous dress no-one her age has the right to look so good in, when Tom prepares to light the Chinese lantern.

A hush suffocates the conversation.

"Happy fiftieth, Sylvie." Tom's voice cracks. "If only you'd lived to celebrate with us. But we're all here – just as I know you'd have wanted – even if the accident has meant you couldn't be."

As everyone claps, the lantern drifts like a dying breath on the breeze.

But I can't see it… everything's misty as I think of Sylvie and how beautiful she'd have looked this evening and how I wish that when I searched, I could see her just one last time…

Suddenly I feel a touch on my arm. It's Tom, shadows under his dark eyes.

"So you came after all, Carla?"

I nod, tears skating my cheeks. He pulls me into a bear hug. Then, holding me away, he looks into my eyes.

"It was only a tiff. Sylvie laughed about it before she left that… day. Said she'd call you later to apologise."

"I only wanted to warn her that being late might mean she'd speed. She took it the wrong way…"

"She loved you, Carla – always had done, always would. You knew her all her life and you had dozens of squabbles. They meant nothing, didn't they?"

"Well, yes…"

"Then so did this one. She was over it. And so should you be, too. Promise me that you are. For my sake and Sylvie's."

Slowly, I nodded. He was right.

"Oh – and Carla, she'd want you to have her dresses. Not yet, but when I'm ready – will you take them?"

Of course. It would be a way of keeping her close.

I nodded and then we all held hands and watched in silence as Sylvie's Chinese lantern slowly drifted away out of sight.

THE AUTHOR SAYS… "A good friend of mine told me about a birthday barbecue he'd attended – with a twist. It gave me the foundation for this story."

Happily Ever After

Weddings are like a fairytale to a child – but more like a bittersweet fantasy to her heartbroken mother...

By Rosemary Hayes

M elissa paused before she read the final line of the story to her daughter; but then that wasn't fair. Why should she spoil her daughter's expectations just because she no longer believed in fairytale endings herself?

"And they lived Happily Ever After," she declared, leaning over to kiss her daughter's forehead. "Goodnight."

"Night, Mummy," Chloe muttered, tottering over the edge into sleep.

Melissa put the dog-eared book back on the shelf and headed to the kitchen. She switched the kettle on and pulled one cup out of the overhead cupboard.

One. It wasn't the only reminder of her new life as a single woman. There was the empty stillness in the air after Chloe had gone to bed; doing all the chores by herself instead of having someone to share them; and there was all that cold space in the queen-sized bed every night.

She took her coffee to the lounge and put the TV on but she couldn't concentrate. All she could think of was Kirk and how she missed him.

She forced herself to think of happier things, such as her cousin's wedding next week at which Chloe would be a flower girl, but it was no use.

She'd met Kirk eight years ago. One Saturday she had been on her morning bicycle ride when a car almost ran into her. Swerving, she fell onto the verge.

Kirk, who had been driving in the opposite direction, stopped to help. He put her bike into the back of his four-wheel drive, drove her to hospital and stayed until she was given the all-clear to go home on crutches with a sprained ankle.

Kirk drove her home and asked her out. She didn't hesitate. It wasn't just his kind nature and amazing smile – wasn't another reason because he had come to her rescue, just like in the fairytales?

They'd married two years later and Chloe was born exactly one year after that. Melissa couldn't have been happier. She had a wonderful husband, a delightful daughter, and a beautiful home they rented close to the city.

Then the IT business Kirk worked for found itself in financial difficulties and **Continued overleaf**

At last it was time for Chloe to put on her beautiful cream satin dress

Kirk was made redundant. After that, one thing after another seemed to go wrong. She knew Kirk found it difficult to express himself, but communication all but ceased.

Six months ago she and Chloe moved to this small flat. Despite the circumstances Melissa was determined to make Chloe's life as wonderful as possible. She was so happy when her cousin Jenny had asked Chloe to be a flower girl. It had given them both something to look forward to.

The only problem was, Kirk was one of the groomsmen, but Melissa pushed her mixed feelings aside.

On the morning of the wedding Melissa had never seen her daughter so excited.

"Can I put my dress on now?" she squeaked after breakfast.

"Not yet. We'll go to Jenny's after lunch with antique ribbon. She thought Chloe couldn't possibly look any more radiant – until the horse- drawn carriage pulled up.

"Mummy! Mummy!" Chloe jumped up and down, clapping her hands. "Jenny said I'll be going with her in the carriage, with horses. Just like a real fairytale princess."

Melissa's heart ached.

"That's wonderful. I'll meet you at the church. Now do exactly what Jenny says."

Melissa slid into a pew at the church. Most of the guests had arrived and the groom and groomsmen were already waiting at the altar.

She couldn't help glancing at Kirk as he stood with the other groomsmen. He met her gaze. She couldn't read the expression on his face but for some reason her heart quickened and she looked away.

Just then the wedding march started

Seeing Kirk and Chloe together, it was hard not to feel regret and longing

– that's when you and Jenny and the bridesmaids will start getting ready."

If the morning had passed with agonising slowness, the afternoon whizzed by in a blur. Melissa kept an eye on her daughter as the wedding party was primped and pampered. Chloe's dark hair was styled into a French bun and threaded with flowers, lip gloss was applied, and a manicurist applied clear nail polish.

"*Now* can I put my dress on, Mummy?" Chloe's eyes were sparking like jewels.

"Yes, Chloe. Now you can."

Tears threatened as Melissa helped her daughter into her cream satin dress which fell to her ankles and was tied at the waist playing and everyone turned to watch the bride enter. Chloe walked in first, carrying a basket filled with rose petals which she sprinkled carefully down the aisle. Next came two bridesmaids in blue silk dresses. Behind them Jenny and her father walked slowly, savouring every moment.

Melissa only had eyes for Chloe, who was obviously having the time of her life.

At the reception venue Chloe gasped when she saw the large sweeping staircase leading to the cavernous decorated ballroom. Chandeliers hung from the ceiling, tables were adorned with flowers, crystal glasses and gold-edged plates.

"Mummy, is this a fairytale?" she asked.

Melissa was about to say, "No, it's just a wedding", but then decided that maybe for one night it wouldn't hurt to see through her daughter's eyes.

"Maybe it is."

The reception went perfectly. The food was scrumptious, the speeches short. Watching Kirk and Chloe across the room, hugging, talking and laughing, it was hard not to feel regret and longing.

The music started.

"Would you like to dance?"

It was Kirk. When was the last time she had been in his arms?

She took his hand and they danced. Finally Kirk broke the silence.

"Chloe's beautiful – she takes after you, obviously."

Why did she have to be so aware of his body close to hers? She noticed Chloe watching them and waved.

"She thinks she's in a fairytale. I haven't the heart to tell her there's no such thing."

"There isn't?" Kirk held her tighter and looked into her eyes. Melissa felt dizzy.

"This wedding has brought back so many memories of our special day," he whispered. "I remember how beautiful you looked, I remember the vows we made… for better or worse."

"Looks like we didn't manage to make it through the 'for worse' bit, did we?"

"That was my fault," Kirk admitted. "I didn't deal with redundancy very well. I felt like I'd let you down. I couldn't give you and Chloe everything you deserved."

"But we didn't need expensive material things, all we needed was you. I tried to tell you but you shut me out."

"And I was wrong to do that. I should have said this long before now, but I'm sorry. When I saw you in the church today, looking just like you did the day we got married, I knew I'd do whatever it took to make it up to you, and to Chloe. All these months apart, I've never stopped loving you."

"I never stopped loving you either," Melissa admitted.

Later that night as her mother tucked her into bed, Chloe yawned and said, "It was just like a fairytale, Mummy – and when you and Daddy danced together you looked just like a princess and a prince."

"Did we?"

Chloe nodded.

Melissa remembered the midnight kiss she and Kirk shared tonight. Afterwards they agreed they would see a marriage counsellor together and give their relationship the second chance it deserved.

Melissa may still not believe in Happily Ever After just yet, but for now, she liked the sound of To Be Continued....

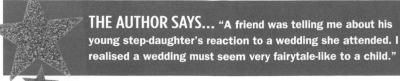

THE AUTHOR SAYS… "A friend was telling me about his young step-daughter's reaction to a wedding she attended. I realised a wedding must seem very fairytale-like to a child."

ILLUSTRATIONS: SHUTTERSTOCK, MANDY DIXON, THINKSTOCK

Prince Charming

Really? Surely not! But yes, it seemed a Royal would be opening the village Art Group exhibition...

By Linda Gruchy

Liz Parker gave a heavy internal sigh as she glanced around the members of the committee of the Runworthy Art Group.

They were discussing the group's forthcoming art exhibition and she wondered if she was wearing the same fixed, polite expression as everyone else as they listened to Madam Chairman Mrs Forbright holding forth.

When Liz had first joined the Art Group six months ago she'd misheard the name as "Mrs Forthright", which seemed appropriate for a woman who took no prisoners in the quest to get her own way.

Mrs Forbright was droning on about getting someone famous to open the exhibition, asking the committee for suggestions, leaving six seconds for replies before continuing with her own ideas – which, if previous committee meetings were anything to go by, would be accepted meekly and merely ratified by the rest of them.

It's your own fault you're here, Liz chided herself. *If you hadn't let on about your computer or told them about you being a retired secretary, they'd never have co-opted you onto the committee.*

Co-opted wasn't quite the word, really. Inveigled, more like, or even, steamrollered. Committees were like that, nowadays, Liz supposed; run by a few stalwarts while the rest ducked like rabbits when a buzzard soared overhead.

She mentally sniggered at the image of Mrs Forbright as a buzzard; those piercing eyes over that beak-like nose. Once she'd got her claws into someone...

A change in atmosphere dragged Liz out of her reverie. Oh no. She'd obviously missed some question or other. She felt the same terror as when, many years ago, she'd been put on the spot by the scary headmaster, asked a question she hadn't even heard through daydreaming.

"I think it's a great idea," said Len.

One by one the committee assented to whatever the question had been.

"Fine by me," said Liz, hoping she wasn't letting herself in for some chore or other, like baking a huge fruit cake or half a dozen quiches. If only she'd heard the **Continued overleaf**

A change of atmosphere ended Liz's reverie. What had just been said?

Continued from previous page

question. Still, if she had inadvertently volunteered for something, it would be in the Minutes. Sally, the minutes secretary, was scribbling away (unless that was a doodle she was working on so assiduously).

"Well that's settled," declared Mrs Forbright with a satisfied nod. "Prince Charles it is, then. If you could deal with that, please, Sally."

Liz heaved a sigh of relief over not accidentally volunteering to make three dozen quiches and a half-ton fruit cake, but surely she'd misheard. Prince Charles would be opening their art exhibition?

Before the meeting broke up, she found herself committing to two Victoria sandwiches, and to do the teas at the opening ceremony.

When she got home, Liz settled herself down with a cup of tea. So, HRH Prince Charles was going to open their exhibition, was he? How exciting!

It didn't seem quite the thing, but perhaps that was the sort of thing royalty had to do, nowadays, to retain the love of the people.

Not like years ago. Her mind drifted back to Prince Charles' Investiture as Prince of Wales in the summer of '69. She'd seen it on TV, watched the young prince, shy and noble in his stately regalia. He'd looked so valiant, she'd lost her heart to him there and then. She'd remained ever-so-slightly in love with him ever since.

Or at least, the romantic fantasist in her had. In reality, she'd fallen deeply in love with John, married

him and been faithful to him, mind and body, until she lost him a year ago.

She must have misheard what Mrs Forbright said – though she hated to confess it, even to herself. Maybe they'd been talking about someone called Charles who would be exhibiting some prints, or something.

Hello, Elizabeth," boomed the plummy voice over the phone. "Vera Forbright here."

Vera? *Vera?* In all the time Liz had been a member of the Art Group, she'd never heard Mrs Forbright's Christian name being used, to the extent that she sometimes wondered if she actually had one. Perhaps the vicar had taken one look at her as an infant, christened her "Mrs", and dumped her in the do-gooder pew.

Liz moved the phone several inches from her ear, and could still hear "Vera" telling her that she was phoning everyone because the Minutes would be late, not done until after the exhibition, because Sally was ill. Was Liz still all right for Victoria sandwich cakes and to help Leonard and Sally with the teas?

By the time the phone call ended, Liz had promised three rather than two Victoria sandwiches, made with sieved jam because those horrid pips got under people's false teeth plates, and she'd agreed that two dozen butterfly cakes would be a Very Good Idea.

Why? she thought as she put the phone back into its cradle. *Why did I say yes? I bet the rest bring packets of digestive biscuits and feel they've discharged their duty.*

What to wear, that was the problem. A pretty floral dress, perhaps, something soft and feminine?

Perhaps not; Mrs Forbright had a tendency to wear floral prints and Liz didn't want to look as if she were competing – particularly as her figure, though now comfortably padded, was far better than Mrs Forbright's. Vera Forbright looked like a frigate in full sail when she was on her feet, and just as majestic. It wouldn't do to be a sleek schooner beside her.

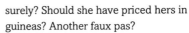

Yet if Prince Charles, her hero, was to be there, Liz really ought to make the effort. Perhaps she should treat herself to something new.

Don't you think one hundred pounds a little steep for your watercolours?" Mrs Forbright sniffed at Liz as she hung her pictures in the exhibition venue.

surely? Should she have priced hers in guineas? Another faux pas?

She had a quick flick through the catalogue, relieved to find that the others were mainly priced in pounds, though her paintings were the highest priced of everyone's.

Nobody was going to buy hers, not at that price. But that didn't matter because Liz was worried nobody would buy them even if they were priced at a fiver – and a price like that would have seemed desperate.

She slipped off home to get into her new ensemble. She was thrilled with it; a pleated skirt which ended below the knees, hiding what she considered to be her worst points, and showing off her best attributes, her still-elegant ankles. She'd found some miraculously comfortable court shoes and a handbag to match. She had a top of rich golden silk which clung in all the right places, and a rather trendy-looking jacket

"Oh, he's here already," said Len. "Having sherry with Her Ladyship"

Mrs Forbright's oils were stolid executions of chrysanthemums which she had priced at fifty guineas – which, she went on to tell Liz, barely covered the materials.

"I was going to charge twenty pounds, but my daughter said nobody respects a low price tag, and insisted," said Liz mildly, mentally making a note to look up "guineas". As far as she was concerned they were in the same league as gold doubloons or pieces-of-eight.

Nobody paid guineas nowadays,

which made her feel young and glamorous without feeling absurd.

Len was in the exhibition kitchen when she got back, laying out cups and saucers.

"Wow," he said appreciatively.

"When's Prince Charles coming?" asked Sally as she joined them, dumping another cake on the countertop. She gave a little giggle and smoothed her hair. She had obviously recovered from the lurgy.

"Oh, he's here already," said Len. "Having sherry with her ladyship."
Continued overleaf

Continued from previous page

"Her Ladyship?" asked Liz. Seemed like something else had passed over her head during her daydreaming.

"He means Mrs Forbright," said Sally with a laugh.

"Oh, thanks, I see," said Liz, her heart beginning to thud with pleasure. It was true, then; she hadn't misheard. Prince Charles was actually here. If Mrs Forbright was a Ladyship, that might explain how she managed to get Prince Charles to come. She probably knew him personally. Or maybe Camilla was a chum of hers.

"How does one address him?" Liz asked in a sudden panic, wishing she'd thought to practise her curtsies.

"I believe the correct form is to say, 'Your Royal Highness' on first acquaintance, and 'Sir' thereafter," said Len. "He's going to have a private viewing before we open to the public. Her ladyship is making a right old game of it, going to call us up one by one to be presented with

and suddenly there he was – Prince Charles, in the flesh, with Lady Forbright in full sail beside him, Sally hovering like a lady-in-waiting.

Liz wondered why he had no bodyguards. Surely he should have a protection team making sure nobody slew the Next-in-Line with a palette knife?

Liz had never seen Prince Charles for real before and she thought him even better-looking than the photographs or TV suggested. No wonder she'd fallen in love with him all those years ago. He looked just as scrumptious now in that mid-grey suit of his.

She was rather perturbed at the lack of reverence shown by everyone else. Surely they should curtsy or bow when presented by Her Ladyship?

"Mrs Elizabeth Parker," called out Sally. Liz walked on trembling legs over to the Prince and Lady Forbright, curtsied, and – oh my – shook Charles' hand.

"Lovely, lovely paintings," he said in

He was so handsome. No wonder she'd fallen for him all those years ago

our paintings. Just a chance to preen if you ask me." Len chuckled.

"Oh give over," said Sally. "She might be as unstoppable as a tsunami but she works hard for us. She gets things done."

"That's true. This is amazing," said Liz with a shiver of glee.

"Oh gosh, I'm supposed to be with them, calling out names like some posh dinner do," gasped Sally. She scuttled off. Liz and Len continued to sort out the cakes.

The door into the anteroom opened,

that instantly recognisable voice. "I'm very keen on watercolour as a medium," he added.

"I know," squeaked Liz. "You paint in watercolour yourself, don't you, Sir?"

Charles looked momentarily nonplussed before saying, "Ah yes, quite so, quite so." He lavished praise on her paintings, with that lovely hand gesture he was wont to use, while Liz listened, enraptured, the breath stolen from her lungs.

All too soon, it was time for Charles to move on to the next exhibits. "Perhaps

we'll speak later," he said as his eyes travelled down to her ankles.

When the VIP guest had looked at all the paintings, the public were admitted.

"Lots more than last year," observed Len in surprise.

"That's because Mrs Forbright sent them special invitations," said Sally peevishly. "That lot are her friends."

Soon they were busy serving tea and cakes to a multitude of people and there was a pleasing hubbub of voices.

There was a sharp rapping of Vera Forbright's walking stick on the floor. She made a mercifully short speech, then invited Charles to open the exhibition and present the trophy for the best exhibit.

Liz was miffed because she could hardly see him, since she was in the kitchen and everyone was standing in her view. Worse, she was struggling to hear over the sighs, the coughs and laughter.

Charles gave a very witty speech,

praising the paintings and the venue.

"He's very good," said Len.

"Shhh," said Liz, just as she heard her name. What was that? She turned to the other two.

"Go on," urged Len. "You won the trophy for the best painting. That'll put her ladyship's nose out of joint. Go and be presented with the cup."

On legs that had a mind of their own, Liz tottered over to where Prince Charles and Lady Forbright were standing.

"Many, many congratulations on a lovely piece of work," said Prince Charles, gesturing, and gazing at Liz with light grey eyes. Even as she stammered her delight and thanks, Liz was thinking that she could have sworn his eyes were darker than than in the photos she'd doted over.

The kiss on the cheek really caught her by surprise, such surprise that she almost fainted, and it was only his strong arm suddenly supporting her which prevented a graceless slump to the floor.

"I say – steady on there. Are you all right, my dear?"

"Yes Sir – quite all right, thank you."

Mortified, Liz slunk back to the kitchen and was soon busy serving tea and cakes to everyone.

She was quite surprised to see Prince Charles lingering. She'd expected him to be whisked off by helicopter as soon as the exhibition was opened. He was mingling with the guests and chatting away, then, all of a sudden, he was at the hatch, wanting a cup of tea and one of her butterfly cakes, and asking her to join him at one of the tables – surely she could take a break for a few minutes?

You bet she could.

They walked over to an unoccupied

Continued overleaf

Continued from previous page

table. The conversation was a little stilted until he managed to spill tea on his tie.

"Oh drat," he said. "I hope that comes out in the wash. Do you have any tips on getting rid of tea stains?"

"White vinegar, I think – or beer," offered Liz.

"Thanks – I'll try that. It's one of my favourite ties."

Soon they were gossiping like old friends and Liz found herself relaxing, smiling at him. He was smiling back, smoky eyes alive with amusement and pleasure, even telling her to call him

ought to tear the card up – not look at it, burn it, even. It was wrong, quite, quite wrong, but she turned the card over.

It said, *Charlie Smith, Prince Charles Look-alike; Available for Fetes, Parties and Similar Occasions.*

He's gone, then. Wasn't he great? Just like the real thing." Sally placed two fresh cups of tea and two cakes on the table then plumped herself down into the chair Charlie had been occupying.

"Someone else has taken over tea duties, so we can have a well-deserved rest. What's up? Something upset you?"

It was wrong, so wrong, to lust after the future king – but she did. Oh, yes...

"Charlie". He was so – so *nice*.

He glanced at his watch and winced.

"What a shame, I need to go. I wonder if we might meet up again?" He laid a warm, manly hand on hers. "Could I perhaps take you out to dinner?"

Liz stared at him, jaw falling open.

"Is, is that quite proper, do you think?"

No, no, it was outrageous. Whatever would Camilla think?

"Think about it," he murmured, pressed his card into her hand as he rose, then slipped away.

Liz sat for a full minute waiting for the maelstrom of emotions to subside. It was wrong, so wrong to lust after the future king, but she did. Oh yes, she did. She

"I've been the most awful fool," said Liz, and explained.

Sally giggled. "Did you honestly think he was the real thing?"

"Don't you laugh," said Liz. "I was so deferential, curtseying, calling him 'Sir' and all. I paid a lot for this outfit, and that seems an unjustifiable extravagance now."

"I wouldn't worry about it. Everyone just thought you were really getting into the spirit of it, playing along. The outfit is truly lovely on you. As for this Charlie, well, why don't you take him up on his offer? Find out if the real man is as nice as his make-believe persona."

Liz stirred her tea, looked up and smiled.

"Do you know, I think I might."

THE AUTHOR SAYS... "If you've ever sat on club committees you'll know the temptation to let your mind wander, which is dangerous because you might miss something important..."

FANCY THAT!

Fascinating facts about **India!**

✦ **India is the world's leading exporter of bananas.**

✦ **With a population of 1.2 billion, India is the world's largest democracy.**

✦ **In West Bengal, cows must have a photo ID card.**

✦ Hindu brides choose marigold flowers as a symbol of good fortune and happiness.

✦ **Saying her husband's name aloud is considered disrespectful by many Indian wives.**

✦ Cricket may be India's most popular sport, but the national sport is field hockey.

✦ **Indian beauties have won two Miss Universe and five Miss World titles.**

✦ The game of chess originated in India, where it is called chaturanga.

✦ **The villagers of Shignapur have no front doors on their houses or shops – yet nothing has ever been stolen.**

✦ **Arshid Ali Khan, a 13-year-old boy born with a tail, is worshipped as a god by local people.**

A Kumbh Mela festival in 2001 attracted 60 million Hindus – a gathering so large it was able to be photographed from space.

✦ Holy cow! Hindus treat cows as sacred because they are considered one of humankind's seven mothers.

✦ **Indian police officers are paid more if they grow a moustache.**

✦ Going to an Indian funeral? Wearing white, not black, is considered respectful.

The national animal of India is the Bengal tiger

Sun And Sandcastles

She was back at the beach hut after all these years… but could she turn the clock back for Mum and Gramps?

By Claire Buckle

Forty-nine, fifty, fifty-one… Annabelle squinted, scanning the row of beach huts a little way ahead. There it was, number fifty-two, sandwiched between its smarter, brightly painted neighbours.

Her feet sank into soft, warm sand and her legs and arms, bare in shorts and tee shirt, prickled in the August heat. Yet, as she walked towards the hut, a shiver rippled through her body.

Memories resurfaced of herself, as a child twenty years ago, digging in the sand outside the hut. There'd been angry yelling inside, Mum and Gramps, noisier than the cawing gulls above. Then Mum storming out, hauling her away before she had a chance to pick up her bucket and spade.

A wave of sadness swept over Annabelle as she delved into her bag for the key. The hut's green paint was peeling away in crispy layers, the balustrades surrounding the deck's bare wood were rotting and the scalloped roof trim was broken. The lock was rusty too, but to her

surprise, it took just one shove with her shoulder for the door to swing open.

The previous week, and with a stab of guilt at not having seen him for months, Annabelle phoned her grandfather and arranged a visit to his seaside home. He was waiting at the front door, smiling and waving as she pulled up in the car.

"Not like you, Gramps, to go for designer stubble," she said light-heartedly, giving him a kiss on the cheek. His usually smooth face was whiskery and there was a distinct absence of his favourite sandalwood aftershave.

He rubbed his chin and tutted.

"Must have slipped my mind, thinking about seeing my best girl. Never mind, come through to the study. I've something for you."

"OK," she said, a little puzzled. Usually he'd insist she relax in the lounge while he put the kettle on.

Instead, Annabelle followed him into the small, sunny room overlooking his garden with its neat edges and colourful bedding plants. The smell of beeswax, mingled with the mustiness from Gramps' collection of second-hand books, was familiar and comforting.

He picked up a long, iron key from the mantelpiece and handed it to her.

"Here you are. It's all been sorted out."

The key was cold in her palm.

"What has?"

"Didn't I say?"

She gave a bewildered half-laugh.

"No, Gramps. I've only just got here."

"Ownership of number fifty-two, of course," he announced.

"The beach hut!" Astonishing. He hadn't talked about it in years.

"That's right." He rummaged in the top drawer of his old mahogany desk. "You just sign the document, which is in here somewhere, and it's yours. It's a present for your twenty-first," he said, removing a thin file and placing it down on the desk.

Continued overleaf

He picked up a long iron key from the mantelpiece and handed it to her

Continued from previous page

"For my birthday…?" she said, her eyes widening.

"Yes, yes, your birthday," he answered, sounding flustered. "Sell it if you like. Get out of that rented place and use the money towards buying a flat. My solicitor told me those huts go for a small fortune. Mind you, I reckon it'll need some smartening up."

"Have you been there recently?" she asked, trying to keep her voice calm.

He perched on the edge of his desk. His reply was gruff.

"No. Too many bad memories."

Annabelle was aware she'd need to tread carefully.

"I wish things were different between you and Mum."

Her grandfather's face sagged and his shoulders slumped.

"Let's not talk about Mary and me. At least you wanted to visit."

In her early teens, Annabelle had persuaded her mother to allow her to visit Gramps. After exchanging a few curt words with him, Mary had driven off, swallowed the tightness in her throat.

"Lovely. I could do with a cuppa, Gramps. And next Saturday I'll have a proper look at the hut."

Wrinkling her nose at the stale smell, Annabelle propped the door open with her bag. The hut was stifling, as though all the air had been sucked out, and it was good to feel a breeze on her face. Sunlight tumbled in, illuminating a haze of dust motes.

When Annabelle was tiny, her mother would have told her it was fairy dust. She could almost hear Gramps teasing saying, *away with the fairies, more like*.

A child's fishing net stood in the corner. On the floor, a tin bucket depicting frolicking children lay on its side. Both triggered a pang of nostalgia. She'd used them to catch tiny iridescent fish in rock pools.

"Drops of a rainbow fell into the water, that's why the fish are so pretty," she remembered Mum saying when she showed off her catch.

"You fill that child's head with a lot of

She remembered her mum's words – Make a wish, there's magic in that shell

leaving them alone together.

"Welcome back, my best girl," Gramps had said, his eyes brimming with tears.

That was the start of the close bond that had grown between them.

Gramps' voice cut into her thoughts.

"Now, how about a cup of Earl Grey and some hazelnut cookies?" he said and winked cheerfully.

Annabelle smiled. He always remembered to buy her favourites. She nonsense, Mary," Gramps had grumbled.

Annabelle had wondered whether to tell Gramps she knew Mummy was making it up. She'd sometimes pretend they were princesses living in a castle, decorating their dingy rented flat with swathes of cheap muslin draped around the curtain poles and budget fairy lights looped across her headboard.

Two deck chairs lay folded on the floor. The faded blue fabric was dusty, fraying at

the edges and laced with cobwebs. She had a vague image of Gramps sitting in one as she built sandcastles at his feet. Was he dozing or reading?

Her mum was probably sitting in the other one, no doubt curling strands of her long, fair hair round her finger while immersed in a romantic paperback.

She turned to the one piece of furniture in the room, a three-drawer chest; its cream paint tinged to an aged yellow. A couple of knobs were missing along with one of the feet, causing it to tilt.

The top drawer contained just a few shells. She picked one up. Large and gently curved, its inside gleamed like mother of pearl. She closed her fingers around it remembering her mum's words.

Make a wish, there's magic in that beautiful shell.

She pulled out her phone from the pocket of her shorts.

I think it's tragic that you two won't talk," Annabelle said to her mother. They'd met in the park and were sitting on a bench, shaded from the sun by a weeping willow. The sweet scent of cut grass drifted around them. The sound of children playing carried on the light breeze.

Mary snorted.

"My father has never understood me and never will. Considering he was artistic and a Pisces, he's always been insensitive to my feelings."

"Artistic?"

"Doesn't he still draw?"

Annabelle frowned.

"I don't think so."

"Oh, well, he used to." Her mother's eyes misted over. "I know he struggled after Mummy died and it must have been hard bringing me up on his own. I was just twelve, you know, when she had the stroke."

Annabelle nodded; she had heard the sad story on many occasions.

"But even so," her mother continued briskly, "he expected too much of me. I was never academic but he nagged at me to do well at school."

"You can't blame him – you did the same to me. Besides, he stood by you when you got pregnant," Annabelle said.

"Hmmm."

"Come on, Mum, you were only sixteen. He must have been pretty upset."

"Can we drop the subject, please?" her mother replied, but Annabelle persisted.

"No, we can't." her jaw tightened. "He's given me the beach hut."

"Really? That old thing?"

Annabelle grasped her mother's hand and gave it a little shake.

"Yes, really. For my twenty-first birthday."

That caught Mary's attention.

"But it was two years ago."

Continued overleaf

Continued from previous page

"Exactly. It's obvious he's getting confused and starting to have problems with his memory. I know you were close before that argument. Why haven't you ever made up?"

Annabelle felt her mother pull away.

"For goodness' sake, we've been through all this before. Gramps was angry when I went back to your father after we split up. I thought if I told him while we were at the beach, he wouldn't make a scene, but I was wrong. He was so unreasonable because…" Mary's cheeks flushed a bright pink.

Annabelle felt a lurch in the pit of her belly. "Because of what? Tell me."

But Mary clamped her lips together as though the words were trying to escape.

"Mum, Gramps has been lost to you for all these years. Don't give up on the chance to find him again before it's too late," Annabelle pleaded.

Her mother's body seemed to deflate and she exhaled heavily.

"All right, I suppose it's time you knew. Dad and I split up and then got back together after…after he lost the money Gramps had given us."

Annabelle's mouth went dry.

"What money?"

Her mother twisted the silver ring on her thumb and stared into the distance.

"You're right. Gramps was shocked when I became pregnant but after a while he accepted that Richard and I wanted to be together. He rented a little cottage for us. Dad had just finished his decorating apprenticeship and didn't earn much. We had you, got married and then, when you were about four, Gramps gave us thousands of pounds towards a deposit for a place of our own."

In a whisper, Annabelle asked, "How did Dad lose the money?"

Her mother bit her bottom lip.

"A so-called friend convinced Dad to give him the cash to invest in some sort of scheme buying and selling land. Told him he'd double the money almost immediately. Within a week he'd disappeared with the lot. I was livid Dad had gone behind my back so I fled with you, to Gramps'."

Annabelle felt herself welling up.

"I never knew why, but I remember us staying with Gramps that summer."

"He was devastated," Mary continued. "The only other time I'd seen him cry was when Mummy died. He said it wasn't just the money. What he couldn't understand was how Dad had been so irresponsible towards his family.

"Gramps told me he'd look after us, that we should have nothing more to do with your dad and I agreed. I wanted Richard to suffer."

"But Dad persuaded you to go back,"

Annabelle said, stating the obvious but desperate to know all the details.

Mary nodded.

"He phoned every day when he knew your grandfather would be at work. Begging… saying he loved us, couldn't bear to be apart, that he'd work twenty-four hours a day to earn enough to support us and never risk our livelihood again. I knew that, despite everything, I still loved him.

When we rowed in the beach hut Gramps said I must be even more stupid than he ever took me for. That hurt. I knew I'd disappointed him and probably,

"I should think it does. It wasn't exactly in pristine condition years ago." Mary managed a weak smile.

"So…" Annabelle let the word linger. "Why don't you come? What do you say?"

Annabelle was kneeling, tugging at the bottom drawer of the chest when a shadow fell across the floor.

"Mum!" she cried, jumping up and flinging her arms around her mother.

Mary hugged her daughter.

"I know I said I wasn't sure if I would come, but Dad and I had a long heart-to-heart and decided it was time."

"I'm going down to the hut. Gramps said it might need a bit of work"

whatever I tried to do, I always would."

She wiped her tears with a tissue and they sat in silence for a few moments. Annabelle tried to imagine her thrifty, steady dad being so naïve.

"Did you get any of the money back?" she asked.

"No, we went to the police, but that man was never found. Probably scarpered abroad somewhere. As for Gramps and me, the years passed and it got harder to make amends. I'm sure he still thinks I'm a total failure."

"That's not true. I've told him you're training to do something you love. And I've said how nice your flat looks now Dad's finished doing it up." She put her arms around her mum's shoulders and gave them a reassuring squeeze.

"I wonder…" Annabelle ventured. "I'm going down to the beach hut next weekend. Gramps says it might need a bit of work."

They drew apart. She raised her eyebrows and shook her head.

"This place has deteriorated something shocking."

"It is a bit of a state," Annabelle agreed, with a deep sigh.

Her mother broke into a wide smile.

"So – it's a good job your dad's got next week off."

Annabelle's stomach did a victory flip.

"That's brilliant. Good old Dad."

"And I've brought some essential oils. Lavender and rose. They dispel negativity, you know," Mary announced, unscrewing a small bottle. Annabelle inhaled.

"They smell delicious."

"It's nice to put my aromatherapy training to good use."

"Perhaps it's worked some magic," Annabelle said, kneeling down and easing the stubborn drawer back and forth. Gradually, it opened.

Continued overleaf

Continued from previous page

"Hey, what's this in here?"

She lifted out a sheet of paper – a pencil sketch of Mary, in a flowery sundress, sitting in a deck chair, engrossed in a book. Her long hair fell in loose curls around her face. At her feet Annabelle, in a swimsuit, was digging in the sand. Ringlets sprung from underneath her floppy hat. In the bottom right corner was Gramps' signature and the title, *My Two Best Girls*.

Annabelle handed it to her mother.

"I've never seen it before," Mary said, her voice catching.

Realisation dawned on Annabelle. Gramps wasn't reading or dozing on that

"One thing's for sure. There's no way I'm going to sell Marybelle's..."

summer's day, but sketching.

"There's something else," Annabelle said. She reached to the back of the drawer and pulled out a pale grey driftwood sign on which MARYBELLE'S was painted in white, perfectly crafted capitals.

Annabelle stood up, "Mum, look."

Mary gasped.

"He must have made it for the hut years ago. And I always thought of him an so unsentimental."

"One thing's for sure," Annabelle said. "There's no way I'm selling Marybelle's. I want to keep it to use when we visit

Gramps. I reckon it's about time he came back down here. Don't you, Mum?"

"Yes, love, I do," Mary agreed.

Annabelle checked her watch.

"That's a relief," she said, feeling a tingle of anticipation, "because I made a phone call earlier and…" She looked out through the open door. Gramps was striding up the beach, waving as he approached.

She glanced at her mother, wondering what her reaction would be.

Mary hesitated for just a moment before she waved back and hurried out of the hut to meet him.

THE AUTHOR SAYS… "The story was inspired by a nostalgic trip to a Cornish beach, where my grandparents' hut once stood. Unlike Annabelle's, my visit unlocked happy memories."

Brain BOOSTERS

Sudoku 1

				1				
		6		8	4	5		
				2				
			8		7	4		
	9			5				
8		4		3	9			1
	7	5		1	9			2
	2		8					
	1		2		6	3		9

Sudoku 2

	9					2		
		5		4				
			6	1		5		4
5	8	9	4					
		3				1	2	
		7	3		5	9		
3			7	9	4		8	
					6			1
		4			3			

Fill in each of the blank squares with the numbers 1 to 9, so that each row, each column and each 3x3 cell contains all the numbers from 1 to 9.

Word Wheel

You have ten minutes to find as many words as possible using the letters in the wheel. Each word must be three letters or more and contain the central letter. Use each letter once and no plurals, foreign words or proper nouns are allowed. There is at least one nine-letter word.

AVERAGE: 36 words
GOOD: 37-54 words
EXCELLENT: 55-71 words

At The Sign of The Bear

What started as ghostly singing set in motion a chain of events that would be talked of for years to come...

By Sandra Morgan

N ot long before the Second World War, my parents took on an ancient Bristol city inn called The Rugged Staff and Bear in Little Peter Street. It came with a resident ghost.

Had she been some malevolent spirit she would have scared me witless, but all our lady did was croon gentle lullabies, unseen, from the dank, cobwebby cellar.

Her voice was high and sweet, like a distant bell, conjuring up images of an ethereal creature from an enchanted world, rather than some menacing spectre.

It was Arthur, the landlord of The Cat and Whistle down the road, who eventually provided a clue to the mystery. He was interested in local history, and

within those very medieval walls. The Inn is said to conceal a secret beneath its well-trodden floors: a cave, from which descends a tunnel to the wharf, reputedly the haunt of long-dead smugglers.

As the wharf slipped into disuse over the years, houses have colonised its deep frontage. Somewhere, lost in their environs, lies the entrance to the tunnel.

Me, well, I'd always believed there was a rational explanation for our warbling spirit, but Arthur's discovery set questions buzzing around my head. Before I could pay them much heed, there was desperate news.

On Sunday September the third, deceitfully gay with sunshine, I joined Mum and Dad around the wireless for Neville Chamberlain's address. When his grave voice drew to a close, with the

I'd always believed there was a rational explanation for our warbling spirit

showed us a flowery piece on The Bear he'd come across:

This welcoming but mildly ugly hostelry reminds one of a genial, crouching gargoyle. Built in 1653, when castle walls protected the city, The Bear and Rugged Staff is recorded as lying

promised peace in our time shattered, Winston Churchill's dark growlings of war had become stark reality.

At six that evening, when King George called upon his people to stand firm and united, I felt a new and powerful sensation
Continued overleaf

The Rugged
Staff and Bear

Fine Wines and Ales

pulsing through me: patriotism.

"I told you Churchill was right all along." Dad's voice quivered with emotion. "Now we'll show 'em."

Mum rounded on him, colour mounting in her cheeks. "With what? Our boys' lives?"

I thought of lads I knew, too young to carry guns. I remembered a quote I once read: *little girl, someday they'll give a war and nobody will come.* I knew already it wouldn't be the way of this one.

Mum was away the following weekend visiting her sister Nance down Dorset way in the small village of Salway Ash, leaving Dad and me at The Bear.

Going into the bar, I almost tripped over a hefty lump hammer and pickaxe lying on the floor.

Dad darted in with his customary economy of movement, clutching a lantern and matches in his hands, mischief written all over his moon face.

"What's that for?" I asked, puzzled.

He winked. "You'll see."

"Mum will hit the roof." I began to enjoy myself.

He kissed my cheek. "She'll come round."

Arthur bellowed laughter, making me jump. "Hah, it'll be a while afore you're 'auled to that pillowy bosom again, Gilbert."

"Children present, Arthur." Dad went slightly pink.

"Sorry, mate."

"I'm sixteen," I huffed. "Not a child."

Arthur turned solemn. "Don't wish bein' grown-up on yourself, Doreen. It'll 'appen soon enough in these sorry times."

As it turned out, Arthur was right, though none of us could have imagined why in our wildest dreams.

Minutes later, we were all crouched in the vast cellar, peering at several gaping holes in the far wall where stonework had crumbled away.

"Found 'em yesterday," Dad enthused. "Since Arthur showed us that bit about the

Dad darted in, clutching a lantern, mischief written all over his moon face

I pointed at the tools. "What're they for? Nearly came a cropper, I did."

Before he could answer, the door was flung open and a male voice boomed out from behind, "Anybody 'ome?"

I turned to see Arthur, sleeves rolled up over meaty arms. Spotting the tools, he strode over and hoisted them as if they were feathers. "Let's find this cave o' yourn then, shall us, Gilbert?"

I stared at Dad, feeling my eyebrows mounting to my hairline. "You're not?"

"Aye, we are too." He grinned wickedly and grabbed a long stick from the bar top.

tunnel, I've been exploring."

He thrust the stick into each hole, meeting resistance, until he came to one where it plunged right through.

"That's it. Get the hammer, Arthur."

It only took a few swings from the man's powerful arms to produce a yawning hole.

"Shine the lantern, Dad." I peered in through a settling dust cloud.

The lantern revealed a narrow tunnel of irregular rock formation.

"Let's explore." Without hesitation, Dad scrabbled over fallen bricks, crouching low, lantern extended before him.

Arthur lurched in next; me right behind.

Emerging bent over from the tunnel, we found Dad swinging the lantern around, illuminating craggy, oily-wet walls.

"Would you credit it. We've been living atop a bloody great cave all this time and didn't know it."

"Dad, stop. Hold the lantern still. Look, an opening."

Beneath jutting rock shelves, I hunkered down, smelling dank river air. "It's the smugglers' tunnel. Got to be."

It all began adding up then. I couldn't understand why it hadn't before.

"Wouldn't the tunnel act as a kind of amplifier for sounds from the wharf? Then wouldn't it carry on through that hole in the cellar wall? Couldn't it explain the ghost?"

Arthur scratched his big bald head, while Dad pondered, frowning so hard his bushy eyebrows knitted together like one of those furry caterpillars.

I jumped up impatiently. "Blimey, it'll be Christmas before you two work it out. Look, I need to go and see about something. Might be a while."

Out on the cobbles, bright sunlight had me blinking like a rabbit rousted from its burrow. Then I was off, racing down to the wharf where the River Avon's cloudy expanse was flowing sluggishly beneath Bristol Bridge like Mulligatawny soup. Ragged children played on doorsteps, chattering and laughing.

So what to do next? Knock on doors asking for a woman who sang lullabies by the entrance to a tunnel?

Stupid, stupid; no, I hadn't thought it through at all. Finding the mystery singer

Continued overleaf

was about as likely as Churchill inviting Hitler to pull on his jackboots and come marching on in.

I was still puzzling over it when autumn's reds and golds began tinting the trees. By then, Mum was speaking to Dad again after his little surprise.

As the grip of war tightened inexorably, The Bear's takings fell as the till closed whenever our fighting boys appeared through the door. Mum and Dad saw it as their contribution to the war effort.

One chill October Sunday, Mum and I went along to morning service at St Mary's Church. Towards the end, the vicar announced, "Now our own little songbird, Lily Jackson, will lead the choir in a hymn that has taken on new meaning in these perilous times: *Onward Christian Soldiers.*"

I turned to see a pregnant, flaxen-

She cut me off, chuckling. "What me, love? Look at this lot." She indicated her large brood. "Leaves me no time for singin' in pubs, I can tell you."

"No, what I meant was, there's a tunnel from the wharf up into The Bear's…" I stopped, realising from her bemused expression I might as well have been talking Swahili. I tried again, "Look, can I ask, do you live down on the wharf?"

"For our sins."

"Do you ever sing outside?"

She nodded. "I take a chair into the back yard when it's fine and sing lullabies to the babes."

I felt a thrill of anticipation.

"I don't suppose it's by a tunnel?"

She grinned impishly. "You're a one for strange questions and no mistake."

My face began to burn. "Sorry. I must sound completely daft."

She seemed to take pity on me then.

She grinned impishly. "You're a one for strange questions and no mistake!"

haired figure slipping from a pew where a thin young man sat amongst several fidgeting children.

When Lily began to sing, her lovely soprano soaring movingly over the choir, it sent shivers down my spine, but not simply because of its sublime beauty – it was because I knew where I'd heard that distinctive voice before.

I sought her out in the churchyard after the service. It all came out in a garbled rush.

"I wanted to say I loved your singing and that actually I've heard you sing before… umm… look, this is going to sound really silly, but it was in The Rugged Staff and Bear inn, down in the –"

"Well, now, I do 'ave a nice spot that catches the sun by some ivy and honeysuckle."

I thought how those rampant climbers would intertwine into a dense thicket, concealing anything behind it.

I gazed at her five lively children.

"It must have been a lot of lullabies."

She burst into peals of laughter, patting her swollen midriff. "An' I 'ope there won't be no more after this one, love, I can tell you. Come on, you lot."

I almost chased after her to ask if I could take a look at where she sang, or arrange a time when I could listen in the cellar, but the heavens opened and everyone ran for home. Perhaps I'd see her around, be given another chance.

The nuisance raids – Mum's term for the bombings – increased over the next weeks and I was packed off to stay with Aunt Nance in Salway Ash. I thought of Lily often, and on visits home I heard her once or twice from the cellar, no doubt singing to her new baby.

Then came that brutal, unforgettable day of November the twenty-fourth when Lily sang a different kind of song. I was home visiting, and late morning, with time on my hands, I wandered down into the cellar to listen for her. She always made me think of the song that was on the radio all the time – *Lili Marlene* – and I was cheerfully humming it, little knowing terror was seconds away.

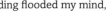

Without warning, there came the scream of bombs falling and exploding, the acrid smell of burning, the crash of masonry collapsing.

Petrified, I tried to run, but my feet were pinned to ground shaking so violently, it seemed it must tear apart.

Then above it all, Lily's voice ascended. *Land of Hope and Glory...*

With her voice my paralysis vanished, and I flew up to the bar, dreading scenes of devastation, picturing Mum and Dad's bodies lying broken and half buried.

But all lay untouched and serene, the only dust in the air, motes that danced in a shaft of sunlight. The bar was as ever at this time – peacefully awaiting customers.

Mum rushed over on her big feet,

hands flapping, pushing a chair under me just as my legs buckled.

"Doreen, whatever? You're white as a sheet, girl."

I heard my own voice, sounding like a stranger's, coming from far away. "Bombs... like the end of the world... Lily was singing."

"No, love." Mum's voice filled with sadness. "We've just heard. Lily died in that last raid." She gave me a hug. "Come on, now, lass. Pull yourself together and let's open up."

I don't know how I helped behind the bar that day, my thoughts spinning in confusion, tears falling for Lily. I wish I'd taken time to take one last fond look around The Bear, because on that day that had lost its lustre, time was running out.

I remember the dull, leaden skies and a light mist before sunset. Funny how clearly such insignificant things etch themselves on memory, when the horror that followed was so ruinous, it crushed the vibrant and historic heart of our city. The Blitz.

The alert came at six-thirty, and soon the city was aglow with flares dropped from enemy planes. As showers of incendiaries kindled and spread, and high explosive bombs whistled and screamed to earth, fires raged, buildings collapsed, and landmarks vanished.

Yet I knew these horrors; they were the ones I'd experienced in the cellar.

Clear as a mountain spring, understanding flooded my mind, and as people fled below skies turned fiery-red, I knew what I had to do. I grabbed a lantern.

"Mum, get Dad. I know what Lily was trying to tell me."

Somehow, we packed the cave with people. In the flickering lantern light, as the ground beneath our feet shook for what seemed an eternity, we sang together – Land of Hope and Glory, challenging the ungodly fury that raged above, and above it all I swear I heard Lily's voice.

When at last silence fell, with dust fallen grey on faces, mothers comforted wailing babes, fathers lowered crying infants from aching arms, hands released hands, and I gave up a silent prayer of thanks to Lily, who'd shown me the way.

She'd doubtless lost her home, as we had, but at least we had our lives.

"Thank you, my dear, from the bottom of my heart," an elderly man whispered. Another tearfully kissed Mum's cheek. Others shook Dad's hand.

Arthur came forging through the rubble, tossing masonry aside. He paused to slap Dad on the back with a bloody hand.

"That was a fine thing you done, Gilbert. So many saved, praise be."

Dad put an arm about my shoulders, his face grey with weariness.

"Here's the one you should thank."

Not long after, I met the young soldier who would become my husband and father of our three sons. Now, all these

When silence fell, I gave up a prayer of thanks to Lily, who'd shown me the way

We emerged a sorry sight, into an alien landscape of raging fires and smoking rubble. Beside a bus half swallowed by a crater, I saw something that broke my heart. Before the ruins of The Bear was the blackened remains of the sign that hung over its door. Still visible was a huge paw clutching a wooden staff.

Suddenly I felt much older. Arthur's prophecy had come true.

Someone squeezed my hand.

"God bless you, Doreen."

Turning, I saw a young neighbour with a grubby, woollen shawl about her sagging shoulders.

years later, we sometimes go into the city, sleekly contemporary without its historic buildings. There's a garden of remembrance that covers the street where The Rugged Staff and Bear stood and a little plaque saying, To All Those Who Lived Here and Lost Their Tomorrows.

If I close my eyes, I can see Mum and Dad behind the bar and hear the trundle of horse-drawn drays on the cobbles.

If I allow my feet to wander below the stairs, I can smell the yeasty aroma of the cellar; and if I wander on, I see a hidden cave that saved many lives.

But most of all I see and hear Lily.

THE AUTHOR SAYS... "My great-aunt and uncle ran The Bear in WW2. Their niece, Doreen, is my mum and she actually met my dad there. They have been married 69 years."

Brain BOOSTERS

Missing Link

The answer to each clue is a word which has a link with each of the three words listed. This word may come at the end (eg **HEAD** linked with **BEACH, BIG, HAMMER**), at the beginning (eg **BLACK** linked with **BEAUTY, BOARD** and **JACK**) or a mixture of the two (eg **STONE** linked with **HAIL, LIME** and **WALL**).

ACROSS

2. Guy, Surprise, Try (4)
7. Bee, Drama, May (5)
8. Choir, Group, Target (8)
9. Acid, Dance, Forest (4)
10. Assistant, Preference, Touch (8)
11. Carving, Pocket, Sharpener (5)
13. Card, Officer, Search (7)
14. Bar, Pigeon, Step (5)
17. Attorney, Lake, Nurse (8)
19. End, Exercise, Picture (4)
20. Fashion, Interior, Label (8)
22. Brush, Poster, Wet (5)
23. Day, Pole, White (4)

DOWN

1. Secret, Spinning, Tank (3)
2. Grand, Insurance, Service (8)
3. Bean, Butter, Powder (5)
4. Climate, Electric, Position (7)
5. Cameo, Comic, Map (6)
6. Cake, Godmother, Tooth (5)
10. Back, Key, Security (4)
11. Machine, Needle, Pattern (8)
12. Emergency, Motorway, Poll (4)
13. Lunch, Model, Party (7)
15. Mirror, Radio, Traffic (3-3)
16. Panda, Slalom, Tortoise (5)
18. Home, Man, World (5)
21. Material, Nerve, Recruit (3)

Cloud Watching

When timid ex-carer Hannah accepts a new lodger, little does she know how her horizons will expand…

By Stella Whitelaw

T his is my home and nothing is going to make me move," declared Hannah, washing flowerpots in the kitchen sink.

Hannah was the kind of woman who pressed flannels with the last of the heat in the iron; vacuumed the garage; wiped the inside of her purse with disinfectant.

This domestication par excellence had evolved from years of caring for a demanding invalid mother. There came a kind of solace in housework and a pride in keeping their home spotless.

When Hannah's mother died peacefully, Hannah picked up the pieces of her life and was able to get her job back at a local firm of solicitors. However typewriters had changed to computers. Letters had become emails. Staff made phone calls on their mobiles. She had to adjust fast.

The house was a late Edwardian villa in a quiet Sussex village, twenty miles from the coast. Hannah kept it so clean, one could eat off the floor.

When the bill arrived for the last few months of private nursing for her mother, Hannah was worried. She needed another source of income.

The front bedroom was a good size, as they were in old houses. Hannah had preferred to stay in the bedroom which had been hers since childhood. This big room was going to waste. The view was going to waste.

She stood by the window and looked at the rolling Sussex Downs, green and wooded, dappled in sunshine, the secretive paths climbing from the foothills into the spine of ridges that in Saxon times had been a royal chase.

Hannah put an advertisement in a local paper: *Large room to let. Suit schoolteacher. No meals. Lovely view.*

The front bedroom was a good size – and the view was going to waste

"No meals" did not sound hospitable, but Hannah had had enough of meals on trays for an invalid. She was through with food. She was thin, not slim.

When a schoolteacher did telephone, it was not quite as Hannah had expected. It was a man. Still, Michael Harris had a pleasant voice and a reassuring manner.

Hannah was impressed when she opened the door to him. Michael Harris was a middle-aged man with brown hair tinged with grey and friendly brown eyes behind heavy-rimmed glasses.

"This is kind of you to see me," he
Continued overleaf

Continued from previous page

said. "Though I feel you are not keen to have a male lodger."

"I thought schoolteachers were women," she said, flustered.

"I teach maths and science."

"Would you like to see the room?"

Michael Harris liked the room. He was enthusiastic about the view and her father's oak desk in the bay window.

"I'd be able to work here," he said. "What could be better than this glorious view? Meals are no problem. I get a good lunch at school. Coffee for breakfast."

Hannah still hesitated.

"I was hoping for a single lady," she murmured.

"I do understand," said Michael Harris. "I should only be here for the school

Hannah discovered that Michael Harris had done a lot of travelling. He talked about teaching in Saudi Arabia, Florida, Israel. It made her solicitor work seem incredibly dull.

He was extraordinarily dutiful to Lenora. He set off in his car every Friday evening, laden with food and wine.

It was not so simple keeping a home spotless with a man around. His feet brought in leaves and mud. His raincoat dripped. The garage began to house tools.

Still, he paid his rent regularly and set off in his car each morning while Hannah cycled to work in the other direction. She rarely saw him.

One evening she bumped into him. She was carrying lampshades that needed washing.

On the quay, small boys fished and the tinkling halliards made mermaid music

week. From Friday evening until Sunday, I shall be away. I spend every weekend, without fail, with Lenora."

"So you are not a bachelor?"

"A bachelor during the week and married to Lenora every weekend." He smiled. "The economics of finding a good teaching post have enforced this separation."

"That's sad," murmured Hannah, deciding. "You can have an electric kettle."

"So that's settled? Is your garage ever used? I'll pay extra for the garage."

"You should sit in the garden," he said. "Watching the clouds. Look what a beautiful evening it is. Your lampshades could wait."

"I have no time to watch clouds," she protested. "This house needs a great deal of upkeep."

Hannah rarely watched clouds, but she did spare a glance as she walked away. Michael Harris was right. They were beautiful rolling billowing cumulus, tinged underneath with rosy pink as they reflected the setting sun's rays.

One Sunday morning, Hannah was faced with the inevitable. There was absolutely nothing to do. Not an inch of her house harboured a mite of dust.

She untied her apron. It would be nice to smell the sea, that fresh ozone. She could catch the midday train to Littlehampton.

An hour later, Hannah stood on the cobbled quayside of the harbour, listening to the murmuring waves, breathing in the salty air. She shifted her bag comfortably on her shoulder and strolled along the quayside. Small boys fished, men messed about in boats, the tinkling halliards made mermaid music. The whole bustling scene was a fascinating world.

She stopped to turn by a small sailing dingy, a rather old boat but well cared-for with its sails neatly furled, the bleached deck washed down, everything ship-shape. There was a man with his back to her and all she saw was a thick seaman's jersey and a navy cap.

She glanced at the name of the boat. *LENORA*.

"Hello," said Michael Harris, looking up. "This is a surprise. We don't often have a visitor."

Hannah was rooted to the spot.

"I thought you went home at weekends. Is your wife here? Lenora?"

Michael looked embarrassed, pushing his cap back.

"This is Lenora," he said. "I never said I had a wife. For better, for worse, in sickness and in health, the commitment is fairly similar."

"You're not married, then?"

"Only to the sea and sailing. It's soothing after a week at school. Why not come aboard and have a look around? Would you like to go for a sail? There's a moderate breeze."

Hannah hesitated. She had never been sailing.

"I'm not dressed for it."

"Soon fix you up. There's a locker full of jeans and jerseys."

Hannah still hesitated.

"I've an outboard motor if the wind drops."

He held out a hand. Taking it, Hannah stepped gingerly onto the moving deck and followed Michael down steps into the cabin. It was narrow, with a single cushioned bench and a small littered table. He opened some locker doors.

"Help yourself," he said. "I'll get the sails rigged. Sorry about the mess."

Hannah reappeared, swamped in a long jersey. She rolled up the hems of the jeans and accepted a yellow life jacket.

Michael could handle the boat on his own. It was exhilarating. Hannah felt a different woman as Lenora sailed out of the harbour.

There were so many new sensations. The slapping of waves against the hull.

Continued overleaf

Continued from previous page

The wind filling the sails with sounds of straining and creaking. The crying of the gulls as they wheeled overhead.

Lenora moved swiftly with the running tide and Hannah's hair soon escaped from its careful knot. It curled in the damp spray and clung to her cheeks.

"Are you enjoying it?" Michael shouted from the tiller.

"It's marvellous." She lifted her face to the sun.

moving about with confidence.

Michael hid a smile. The normally refined Hannah looked like a wild woman of the sea, her hair streaming in the wind, spray on her face and a healthy colour to her pale cheeks.

He jumped ashore at his mooring, secured the Lenora to an iron ring in the concrete and helped Hannah onto the quay.

"Hungry?" he asked.

Hannah looked like a tramp. She could not imagine going into a restaurant.

He had a first class degree, but this was one aspect of life where he was hopeless

As they moved out into the deeper, choppier water, queasiness invaded the hollow of Hannah's stomach. The sea turned from bright blue to troughs of dark forest green. Hannah gazed miserably at the receding coastline of Littlehampton.

Michael arrived at her side with a mug of orange juice.

"Drink this," he said. "It'll help you feel better. The first trip is always the worst."

Hannah sipped obediently. The drink slid down like fire, burning her throat, her lips tingling.

"Whatever is this?" she gasped.

"A well known nautical remedy. A Lenora special."

The Lenora special did the trick. It settled her stomach and by the time Michael turned shorewards, Hannah was

"Stay here," he said. "Watch Lenora for me. All the kids love her."

He returned in no time with several boxes and Hannah found herself sitting on the harbour wall eating fish and chips from plastic containers. She had to admit that she had never tasted anything so delicious.

"I haven't had fish and chips since I was at school," she said. "Mother wouldn't eat anything deep fried."

"There are times when fish and chips are the only thing to eat," said Michael. "After a brisk sail is one of those times.

"I can drive you home," he offered. "When I've secured the boat."

"Thank you," said Hannah. "I could launder those cushion covers for you. They'd be ready for next weekend."

It was the first of many weekends that Hannah went sailing in the Lenora. Sometimes she slept in the cramped cabin while Michael took his sleeping bag into the cockpit under an awning. Gradually she gained her sea-legs and relied less on the Lenora special.

Hannah's Edwardian villa began to look less like a page from a glossy magazine. There were bits of Lenora in the garage being repaired or painted. Wet clothes hung to dry in the kitchen.

Hannah spent her evenings knitting a heavy cable stitch jersey that required immense concentration. Most weekends the house never got a look in. A spider edged tentatively along a window ledge.

"Goodbye, dust," said Hannah cheerfully as she closed the front door.

As they walked along the sea-splashed cobbles of the harbour, Michael broke some news to her. He had seen her change over the weeks and the woman who walked by his side now, her arms laden, was different.

"I have a surprise for you," he said.

He stopped by the stern of a sleek white yacht bobbing gently on the waves, its bows nodding like a white horse. It had shining cabin windows, neat curtains, gleaming brass fitments, a polished teak wood deck. She was spick and span. A haven of spotlessness.

"Lenora has left me," he went on. "She's gone off with a younger man who has the energy to refit her hull. It was love at first sight for both of them. I know he'll take good care of her."

Michael set down his boxes and turned Hannah towards the white yacht.

"What do you think of this little beauty? She's thirty foot long with bilge keels which make her more stable. There's an extra cabin for you and every mod-con. A diesel auxiliary engine will take her anywhere. But she lacks a name."

Hannah saw how the sun was catching the gleaming brass. The pink furrowed clouds seemed to be beckoning the white horses moored at their feet. Was she becoming a cloud watcher, after all?

"She's beautiful," she murmured. "She deserves a beautiful name."

Michael wiped his glasses which had suddenly steamed up. He had a first class degree in maths and science and navigation was no problem, but this was one aspect of life where he was hopeless. He had to know before he got out the paint pot.

"I need your agreement," he said casually. "Shall I call her Hannah?"

Hannah smiled. "What a lovely idea."

THE AUTHOR SAYS... "Walking along Littlehampton harbour, I saw the happiness of small boat owners. This inspired me to write a happy story."

Looking For A Home

Helena may have lost a boyfriend, but a far more amiable companion was about to find her...

By Delta Galton

Helena was drinking tea in her conservatory one sunny evening when she thought she saw a pied wagtail on her bird table.

Seizing the bird book – she was new to this – she looked it up and felt a little stab of pleasure when she saw she was right; black and white feathers and a distinctive wagging tail.

She was so distracted that she dropped the book, which just missed her tea cup. She must be more careful. Colin would not be happy if she ruined his book. In fact, she really should get it back to him.

She put it under the coffee table for safety. It was a pity things hadn't worked

with a few other people for drinks and introduce you?"

Helena had agreed, more for Kate's sake really. She was quite happy on her own, but on first impressions she and Colin had quite a lot in common. He was a keen bird watcher and she'd always liked animals.

He was also good-looking and pleasant company. They'd arranged to see each other again and things had gone well at first. It was only when they'd been out a couple of times that she'd realised they weren't very similar beneath the surface.

She was scatty and a little untidy; Colin got fidgety if all the cups weren't lined up in the same direction on her kitchen shelf, and he went pale if she so much as left an

It was a relief when Colin announced they weren't compatible after three dates

out between them, she thought with a twinge of sadness. Colin was a work colleague of her cousin's, and Kate had been keen they should meet.

"He's a bachelor and seems very nice," Kate had told her. "He's just started work in Purchasing. How about I ask him round

open magazine on the coffee table in his immaculate house. Everything had its place in Colin's world, whereas Helena's world was somewhat haphazard.

It was a relief when Colin announced they weren't compatible after three dates
Continued overleaf

— and that it would be better if they went their separate ways.

Helena was roused suddenly from her musings by movement outside. A sleek black and white cat had just strolled across her balcony. Worried for the birds, she rushed outside, intending to shoo it away, but she was pulled up short.

She could see instantly that her first impressions were wrong. The cat didn't look like a sleek predator any more, just a rather wary kitten, and its ribs could be seen clearly beneath its coat. Its yellow eyes were wary.

"Hello there," Helena said softly, holding out a hand. "Where did you spring from? You look as though you could do with a decent meal."

The cat meowed. It wasn't wearing a collar. Perhaps it had been accidentally shut in a shed and that's how it had got so thin. She'd heard of that happening when people opened up their sheds after the winter. She couldn't recall seeing it before.

Neither had she seen any posters around the neighbourhood reporting one missing. But there had been a Sold sign on the house in the next road for ages. Maybe it belonged to the new owners.

She probably shouldn't feed it, she thought, as she opened a can of tuna. She'd only encourage it. On the other hand she couldn't just ignore it – she'd never had much to do with cats but it was obviously hungry.

The cat wolfed down the tuna. She put some water down too, and it lapped delicately before curling up in a patch of sunlight on the saggy green armchair in her conservatory.

"You can't stay there. I have to go to shopping," she admonished, stroking its head.

The cat purred in disbelief, pressing its head against her fingers, confident of her hospitality. It sounded like a miniature train.

Helena had always thought cats to be independent and feisty creatures, but there was something terribly vulnerable about this one. There was trust in its eyes, which were more gold than yellow, now she looked closely. She supposed it couldn't hurt to let it stay.

When she came back from the supermarket it was in exactly the same spot where she'd left it. She unpacked some tins of cat food and put them away. A line from a song that had been playing on the car radio stuck in her mind. *Somebody called me Sebastian.*

"If you're going to stay, you should have a name," she said. And although Sebastian seemed rather grand for such a slip of a cat, Helena had a feeling he would grow into it.

Over the next couple of days she asked around to see if any of her neighbours had lost a cat. None had. She rang up the local vet and left her details and she even contacted the local radio station, which had a lost and found pets section, in case some child was missing their beloved pet.

No one got in touch. She grew used to having Sebastian around.

He wasn't any trouble. For the next fortnight he came and went. She shut him out when she went to work, but he was usually waiting by the back door when she came home. He'd give a little trill of welcome, half mew, half purr. She started to look forward to seeing him and missed him if he wasn't there.

"You touch that bird table and there'll be big trouble," she told him, but he didn't seem interested in going too close. He was content to sit on the conservatory windowsill and watch the birds flitting back and forth, his head moving like a spectator at a tennis match.

response as he stared at her unblinkingly. Clearly he expected her to help. He didn't seem able to walk on the paw – although she couldn't see any obvious damage.

Alarmed, she bundled him up in her arms and took him to the vet. She didn't have a cat box, but he sat quite calmly on the passenger seat as though he were a seasoned traveller.

"I don't think it's anything serious," said the greying, kind-voiced vet. "Probably just a sprain. Keep him indoors for a few days."

While she was there she asked if there had been any enquiries about him. The vet scanned Sebastian to see if he was micro-chipped, but he wasn't.

Helena wondered if that made him hers. Could you own a cat? She'd once read somewhere that cats owned people, not the other way round.

She bought a litter box and a cat bed, the latter of which Sebastian ignored – he preferred the sofa – and for the next three

Alarmed, she bundled him up in her arms and took him off to see the vet

It made Helena smile. He was also very affectionate, which shattered more of the preconceptions she'd had about cats. He followed her around, twining himself around her legs and leaping up on to her lap the moment she sat down. So much for first impressions, she thought.

And then one day, their comfortable routine was disrupted. It was a Saturday afternoon when he came in meowing piteously and holding up a front paw.

Helena crouched beside him in alarm. "What, sweetie? What have you done?"

She got another sad little mew in

days she kept him in. Luckily it was the weekend. By Tuesday he was walking again with only a slight limp and he took to stalking up and down the conservatory windowsill watching the birds.

With a jolt she found Colin's bird book under a newspaper on her coffee table and realised she still hadn't given it back.

Colin would have evicted you by now," she told Sebastian. "He'd never have coped with cat hair on the furniture."

Sebastian purred incredulously. At the **Continued overleaf** same moment the doorbell rang and Helena jumped. For a moment she thought she must have conjured him up – but it wasn't Colin who stood on her doorstep but a lean, dark-eyed man, with a windswept tangle of hair.

"Can I help you?"

"Do you have a black and white cat?"

"Er, why?" She had an awful feeling he was here to take him away. Perhaps Sebastian belonged to one of his children. He looked as though he might have several – along with a beautiful, bohemian wife.

"I had a phone call from Milford vets – they seemed to think you'd found one?"

"Oh," she said, suddenly wanting very much to lie and say he'd got the wrong house. But she thought of his children and knew she couldn't.

With a resigned sigh, she led him into the conservatory where Sebastian was curled in his usual spot on the sofa.

"The vet told me to keep him in. He hurt his paw, you see. I didn't realise he was yours or I'd have let you know."

Andy looked startled. "He's not mine. Did I say he was mine? He just turned up one day – looked half starved, he did, so I started feeding him. I like cats."

"He doesn't belong to your children, then?" Helena was beginning to think she'd got the wrong end of the stick, especially when the man's eyebrows shot up in alarm.

"Er – no. I don't have any children."

She flushed and turned away.

"Sorry, I just assumed. He's not mine either. He just appeared in my garden one day – terribly thin, like you said."

"So we've both been feeding him."

Andy laughed. It was a warm sound. Everything about him was warm. His eyes, his holey jeans, even his beard – she'd never been keen on them, but this one was framing such a lovely smile.

His first impressions of Andy weren't much better than those of the cat...

He lifted his head when he saw the man and gave a little trill of recognition, half mew, half purr. Helena felt an ache in her throat.

"Hello there, Joker, boy. Hello, old fellow." The sound of purring filled the room as the man stroked his head.

She wanted to weep.

"So his name's Joker," she whispered. "I've been calling him Sebastian."

The man smiled and held out a tanned hand.

"I'm Andy. I live in Fern Avenue – the road parallel to yours. I was worried sick when he disappeared last week."

He stopped stroking the cat.

"You hear about that happening, don't you – the same cat being fed by two people. They're not silly, are they? Actually I've a feeling he may have belonged to the old lady who used to live in my road. She died and I don't think there were any relatives – so maybe no one realised she had a cat."

Before they could ponder this any further, the doorbell rang again. Although ringing it was just a formality, Helena realised, as she went to answer it and saw Colin standing in the hall.

"It was open." He had the grace to

"And this is Andy," Helena added.

"Hmmm," Colin said, and gave her a look which left her in no doubt that his first impressions of Andy weren't much more complimentary than his first impressions of the cat.

"I'll be off, then…"

He backed out of the door, clutching his bird book tightly and shaking his head.

"I hope I haven't made things awkward for you." Andy looked at her apologetically. He filled her kitchen. He looked messy and relaxed and impossibly right there.

"You haven't." She smiled at him. She wanted to say *it doesn't matter if Colin got the wrong impression,* but she didn't because Andy was smiling back and there was a definite hint of interest in his eyes.

blush and she knew he'd come in because he'd heard male laughter. "Sorry if I'm interrupting. Did I leave my bird book here, by any chance? I can't find it anywhere and a friend would like to borrow it."

"Oh, sorry, yes – I meant to call you about that. I think it's in the conservatory, help yourself."

She watched his smile fade as he strolled past her and saw Sebastian.

"What on earth is that?"

"A stray I've been looking after."

"You should be careful – strays can carry all sorts…" He broke off as he spotted Andy, who'd retreated diplomatically into the kitchen doorway.

She was beginning to realise that first impressions were often way out anyway. Her first impression of Colin was that they had a lot in common. She'd been wrong about that. She'd thought Sebastian was a sleek predator, but he'd turned out to be a frightened kitten who'd strolled into her world and so effortlessly stolen a piece of her heart. And by the looks of it, she'd been wrong in assuming that Andy had several children.

She was rather beginning to hope that she'd been wrong to imagine him having a bohemian wife, too…

THE AUTHOR SAYS… "I was inspired to write this story after a chat with a friend about first impressions. We were having a giggle about how often they are wrong."

Hannah's Dress

I had such a close bond with my granddaughter. Yet her girlish longing for the perfect frock rekindled my pain

By Karen Byrom

I t's years since I've been up in the attic of the small bungalow where I've spent all my married life. Since John died, my son-in-law, Greg, fetches down the Christmas decorations and puts them back again.

He and Sandra and my granddaughter, Jenny, come for Christmas every year. It's a tradition that started the year after they were married and they've never missed a year. Greg's parents don't mind – with their big brood, they always have a houseful and Sandra and Greg go there on Boxing Day.

Jenny usually stays with me. When she was little we'd snuggle up together on the

with her schoolfriends at the coffee bar or picture house or ice rink.

I still see her at least once a week. She'll pop round after school to share her latest news, moaning about the unfairness of the French teacher or telling me about the latest "hot" boy in her class. Sometimes, she'll even ask for my help with homework – though I think that's just to make her old gran feel useful. She's headed for university, is Jenny – and oh, I will miss her when she goes.

She was in just a couple of days ago, chattering on about the forthcoming prom night at school for the leavers. That's a new thing since my day – or even her mum's. We had school dances, of course, but they took place in the

She's headed for university, is Jenny – and oh, I will miss her when she goes

couch to drink hot chocolate and watch Disney cartoons. Now she's more likely to be cupping her hands around her mobile phone, Facebooking and appchatting and twitting or whatever it is the young folk do. She's out every weekend, too, as a sixteen-year-old should be, "hanging out"

afternoon and were strictly chaperoned.

I know about school proms of course, from American films and from that TV programme *My Big Fat Gypsy Wedding*, so I was ready with questions.

But Jenny hooted with laughter when I **Continued overleaf**

asked if she had a date for the prom yet.

"Oh, Gran, that's so American! No one goes to school proms here as a couple. I'm going with Hayley, Georgia and Rachel, Geoff, Matt and Joe. It'll be a great laugh.

"Hayley's trying to persuade her dad to take us there in the limousine – can you see snooty Samantha's face when we step out of it? She doesn't know he runs a wedding car company. She's such a snob – she's already on about her dress and how much it cost with all its Swarovski crystals.

"And what are you wearing? A bin bag?" I asked teasingly.

For the first time, her face fell.

"I don't know, Gran," she admitted. "I've been round all the shops and I can't find anything I like. I want a long dress, but nothing too fancy or glitzy."

And then she dropped her bombshell.

"What I'd really like," she said slowly, "is a dress like the one Auntie Hannah wore when she was Mum's bridesmaid. I've always thought it was really beautiful. So simple, just lovely white satin and that great big blue bow. I've looked and looked

in her first long dress, and holding tightly to the hand of Greg's littlest sister to stop her from running out of the photograph.

How well I remembered every minute of that day. How could I not, when just a few weeks later, all our happiness was destroyed in an instant by a joyrider in a stolen car, mounting the pavement where Hannah had just stepped out of the school gates, clutching her clarinet case as she turned back to call a cheery goodbye to her friends.

My baby never stood a chance.

The weeks and months and years went by, and gradually a semblance of normality came back to our lives. John and I were lucky in some ways. Our grief didn't split us up, as it does so many couples. Eventually, I started seeing friends and family again, I even went back to work.

Yet I could never give myself wholeheartedly to anything – until Jenny arrived, five years after the wedding, five long years in which my empty nest had felt emptier by the day, no matter how bright a face I put on it.

No – I couldn't think about it. I had to concentrate on the future we did have

and I can't find anything like it."

"It was a beautiful dress."

My eyes went to the wedding picture that hung on the wall above the dresser. There was Sandra, glowing with happiness in her lacy white gown, clutching a solemn-looking Greg's hand. To her right, Hannah smiled out, a slightly awkward fourteen-year-old, tall and gangly for her age but beaming with pride

Finally, I allowed Johnny to clear Hannah's room, which I'd kept just as she'd left it. Poor Hannah, she'd had that room to herself for just a few weeks, and I had kept it as a sort of shrine to her memory, though I rarely went into it.

Now, John pointed out, we needed it as a spare room for when our new little granddaughter came to stay. I didn't quibble, nor did I feel I was betraying

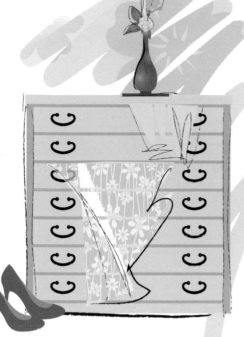

John had cleared the room, but I hadn't been ready to let everything of Hannah's go – and that was why I was now up in the attic, tugging at a large, old-fashioned suitcase and wondering in some dismay how I would ever get it down the steps.

"Hi, Gran!"

Jenny's sweet call saved me from a broken leg or worse. I popped my head down through the ceiling hatch – scaring her out of ten years' growth – and called to her to help me.

Within five minutes we were back in the sitting-room, suitcase on the floor beside us. Sandra, who'd come in just behind Jenny, looked on with a quizzical expression that changed to surprise as I opened the lid.

"Oh, Mum." She leaned forward and picked up the battered purple hippotamus she had bought for Hannah when she was born. At ten years old, she'd waited so long for a little sister. "You kept Hil. I thought you'd got rid of all Hannah's stuff."

"Not all of it," I said, a shade too briskly. I knew if I let a tear fall that she would be in floods, too. We'd cried too much together already. "Just one or two of her favourite toys and some schoolbooks, and a few little trifles of jewellery. Nothing expensive.

"Here –" I dug into the case until my hands closed around an old leather jewellery box, the kind with a little ballerina that would dance when you lifted the lid, and handed it to Jenny. "I can't remember all that's in it, but I know she would have liked you to have anything that takes your fancy."

"Thanks, Gran." Reverently Jenny opened the case and withdrew a pretty **Continued overleaf**

Hannah's memory. She would have adored her baby niece; she loved anything small and cuddly, from her own soft toys to our ancient Cairn terrier, whom she used to smuggle into bed with her at night, despite Sandra's protests.

John and I wouldn't have got a look-in with the baby – although by the time she was born, maybe a nineteen-year-old Hannah would have left home for university or work in another town. She could have been playing clarinet in a national orchestra. Or maybe she would have met the love of her life, even had a baby of her own to love.

No – I couldn't think about it. I had to concentrate on the future we did have. A future that was so much brighter now... even though nothing and no-one could ever replace Hannah.

turquoise ring. "This is so lovely."

"You bought that for her twelfth birthday!" Sandra exclaimed. "I didn't know you'd kept it."

Jenny twirled the ring on her finger.

"I love it, Gran. Thank you."

"Mum, are you sure –?"

I waved a hand firmly at Sandra.

"I'm sure."

Jenny was delving into the case.

"What's this?" she asked, pulling out a card from a slightly yellowed envelope. "Oh, it's a Valentine's card! Auntie Hannah, you sly thing! Who did she get it from?"

"She never would tell me." I shook my head, smiling. "It was the only Valentine she ever got, the February before she… before your mum and dad got married."

"It was from Alan Jones," Sandra said. "Did she really not tell you, Mum? He had a real crush on her."

"Alan Jones? He was twelve! No wonder she didn't want to admit it."

Sandra and I both laughed, but Jenny looked pensive.

"Poor Auntie Hannah. Her only Valentine, from a little boy. I bet loads of boys in her school fancied her. But they just don't send cards at that age," she said with all the wisdom of her sixteen years. "I wish she'd had a chance…"

"Now this won't do!" I said briskly. "We can look at everything later and I'll tell you lots of stories about Hannah. But I brought the case down for a very specific reason – and this is it!"

From the bottom of the case, I pulled out the bridesmaid's dress I had folded away so carefully twenty-one years ago and gently shook out its satin folds.

O h!" Sandra and Jenny gasped simultaneously.

"Oh, Mum…" Sandra put out her hand to touch my arm as together we looked at the dress.

"Oh." My own voice faltered. "I'd thought Jenny could wear it to the school prom. Hannah was so tall for her age that it would fit without much alteration. I hadn't realised…"

The dress, once so pristine, put on with such pride by an excited teenager, was completely yellow.

The satin was cracked in places, and worse, there was evidence that moths had been at work.

"I hadn't thought… Of course, it was so many years ago." My voice faltered.

Jenny and Sandra didn't answer – they didn't have to. We could all see that the dress was unwearable.

Despite all my promises to myself, I couldn't hold back my tears. Hannah's beautiful dress, spoilt. I should have got rid of it years ago.

"It's all right, Gran." Jenny laid a consoling arm around my shoulder. "I'll find a dress. And it was lovely seeing all Auntie Hannah's things. I'll always wear this ring."

Sandra fingered the dress thoughtfully.

wonderful Jenny, so like her aunt in character if not in looks.

"That's a lovely idea," I said, smiling and holding out my hand to Sandra. "But you won't need the blue chiffon." I took up the dress again. "There's nothing wrong with this material – I'll unpick it and you can use it on the new dress."

"Oh, Gran!" Jenny's eyes shone. "It will be nearly as good as wearing Auntie Hannah's dress. Thanks so much." She enveloped me in a hug.

They left, Jenny flashing her new turquoise ring and Sandra carrying the carefully-packaged blue chiffon and a

For a moment my heart was outraged. Then I shook myself. Silly old woman

"You know," she said. "Jenny can't wear this, but there's no reason why we can't make one just the same. There are still two weeks until the prom. Come on, Mum –" she handed me a hankie – "we'll go to John Lewis on Saturday, the three of us, and get some white satin and blue chiffon. If we can't find a pattern, then maybe I could take this dress apart to use for a template."

For a moment my heart was outraged. Take my Hannah's dress apart! Then I shook myself. What a silly old woman I was. My memories of Hannah didn't rest on this old dress, but on all the lovely times we'd had in the past; on her sister, my other beautiful daughter, and on my

scruffy old purple hippopotamus. Why had I never thought she might want a memento of her sister? I shook my head sadly at my selfishness.

Everything else in the suitcase could go to a charity shop. Except the Valentine.

Hannah and Sandra never did discover the truth, that John, acutely aware of his younger daughter's blossoming into young womanhood, had sent it so that she wouldn't have to go in to school and admit she hadn't received any cards. And she'd thought it was from Alan! John would have laughed.

It would be my final memento of them both – that and all their memories, which could never die.

THE AUTHOR SAYS… "Having recently lost a very dear friend, I needed to remind myself that raw grief doesn't last for ever and that happy memories are a legacy more enduring than material things."

Brick By Brick

Oh dear – was Steve's construction project going to lead to the destruction of our relationship?

By Vivien Hampshire

S teve was laying bricks when the argument started. "Are you just going to sit there in the sun doing nothing while I'm slaving away all afternoon?" he said. "It's all right for some, isn't it!"

Well, that was a bit much! I'd spent the best part of the last three hours running around after him – making tea, carrying bricks to him from the pile at the other end of the garden and fetching any tools he needed from the garage. Not to mention the mucky clothes, and the good blanket he'd taken from the airing cupboard to kneel on, that I'd have to wash and iron once he'd finished.

doing the same." I smiled up at him, trying to lighten the mood. "Here, I'll even get you a chair."

But Steve was having none of it.

"No, no, don't you get up, Laura. I don't have the time to laze about in deckchairs, even if you do. And, with my bad back, once I sit down I'll never get up again."

Steve mopped at the sweat on his forehead with the back of a hand and rubbed the small of his back – rather over-dramatically, I thought – with the other.

We'd lived here for almost a year. It was a beautiful little house, with a lovely brick-built extension that had doubled the size of the lounge and added an extra bedroom above.

However the previous owner had left

"No, don't you get up. I don't have time to laze in deckchairs, even if you do"

OK, so I'd settled myself into a deckchair with a cold drink and a magazine, but what was so wrong about that? It's not often we get a sunny Sunday and I needed a break.

"I'm just taking a few minutes' rest," I said. "There's nothing stopping you from

an enormous pile of leftover bricks in the corner of the garden. Quite frankly, I'd got sick of seeing them there and decided it was time we did something with them.

Steve had been keen to build a barbecue. "One of those great big ones **Continued overleaf**

with two grills, and somewhere to rest the plates, and lots of storage underneath."

I think he imagined himself out there every weekend wearing a chef's hat and waving his tongs about, while hordes of friends and neighbours queued up for the privilege of eating one of his legendary burnt burgers and sipping a glass of wine.

With our weather, we'd be lucky to get the chance more than three or four times a year, and the rest of the time I'd be staring at a huge monstrosity of a barbecue taking up far too much space in my pretty little garden.

We'd thought about just dumping the bricks, but moving them all would involve at least five trips to the council tip if we didn't want to ruin the suspension in the car. It seemed such a waste, too. I hated throwing anything useful away.

Anyway, I was feeling in a creative mood. There had to be something we could do with them which would enhance the garden rather than dominate it. What I wanted was a feature, not an eyesore.

That was when I'd come up with the idea of a planter - a low, wide, sweeping trough that I could fill with best-quality compost and a host of wonderful plants. Climbers to hug the fence, bedding plants to add colour, and some nice little trailing things to hang delicately over the front. I could picture it already.

Of course, Steve was dubious about it. We'd only had a small concrete yard at our last place.

"You know I don't know much about gardening," was all he'd said, as he saw his last hopes for a barbecue disappearing in

a virtual puff of smoke. "And the planter thing would need to have curves in it, if you want it to fit in that corner and follow the line of the grass. Curves in brickwork can be quite tricky to do, you know…"

"Steve, I have every confidence in you," I said, and I meant it. If there's one thing my Steve is really good at, it's DIY.

Yes, he cooks breakfast sometimes and helps with the washing-up, and he's even been known to wield an iron when necessary, but mostly we stick to the traditional roles. I like sewing and baking, and making our new home look nice, and he's the sort who enjoys pottering about in the garage, making and mending things. I guess you'd say we complement each other, and that makes us a pretty good team.

So there we were, him muttering under his breath every time a brick didn't sit quite the way he wanted it to, and me trying to enjoy a little sunshine while still managing to offer a few reassuring words and the odd cup of tea.

Steve straightened up, giving his back another ostentatious rub, and surveyed his work in progress.

"Well, what do you think so far?" he asked proudly.

I stood in front of the unfinished planter and cast my eyes along it, Steve standing expectantly at my side.

Inexpert though I was, I couldn't help noticing the mistake.

Well, it was one of those things that, once you'd spotted it, your eyes would just keep coming back to. It stood out like a sore thumb. Among all the rich reds, there was this one little lost brick, a shabby sort of pale, dusty-looking brick, quite clearly a different colour... and already firmly bedded in, four rows down.

I had to tell him, now, didn't I? So of course, that was when the trouble really started in earnest.

"I never wanted to build it in the first make myself go after him. That's the worst bit about arguing – nobody ever wants to back down or admit they might be wrong.

Through the open bathroom window, I heard the shower running for a while, followed by the slamming of the front door. I knew he would have gone off to the pub, to cool off and calm down, but I wasn't going after him. If he expected an apology... well, he was the one who'd made the mistake, not me!

I sighed and sat back down to try to make the most of what was left of the sunshine, but somehow I couldn't get back into my reading. I kept thinking about Steve. Yes, I was upset, and a tiny bit angry too, but I loved him – and oh, how I hated arguing with him!

So the planter wasn't quite perfect. I had to admit there were times when being married felt not quite perfect, too. Just one little thing going wrong could

Perhaps I should just finish the thing myself. That would show him...

place," he said, glaring at me defiantly. "And why does it matter anyway? Who'll notice one brick out of place among all that lot? And what help have you been, sitting there in your chair? If you'd been paying more attention, you could have stopped me as soon as I'd laid it."

Then he threw his trowel down on the grass and strode off towards the house, grumbling, "I wish I'd just gone ahead and built a barbecue after all..."

Oh, dear! I stood and watched him go. I knew I was being too critical, knew I'd upset him, but somehow I just couldn't make the whole relationship feel off-kilter, and it was so much easier to blame each other than it was to say sorry.

Was I expecting too much? Making too much fuss? One odd brick, one really silly argument...

Of course, I kept looking across at it, my eyes going straight to the one place I was trying so hard to ignore. If Steve was going to walk off in a huff, perhaps I should just finish the thing myself. That would show him. Tricky curves, bad back... Huh! I'd watched him all afternoon

Continued overleaf

and it all looked simple enough. And, wouldn't he be surprised? Pleased, even…

So… if I could just get a bit of a practice in, laying a few bricks of my own over at one of the edges, then maybe, once I'd got the hang of it, I could try knocking out the front section and replacing the brick that wasn't right. How hard could it be? There was still plenty of that mortar stuff mixed up, and I knew if it wasn't used quickly it would set hard and be no use at all. I do so hate waste.

Yes, I decided, I would give it a go. All I had to do was get into my old trousers, and don a pair of gardening gloves to protect my nails…

Steve came home a couple of hours later in a much better mood, but that was probably due to the pub atmosphere, a game of snooker with his mates, and the expectation of dinner waiting for him on the table.

He found me in the garden, my clothes, face and a good part of the lawn splattered with dollops of mucky cement, and the oven empty.

"What on earth have you been doing?" he said, trying to suppress a laugh.

"I was trying to help," I mumbled lamely. "But it's not as easy as I thought."

"Had a bit of bother with the curves, did you?"

"I haven't even mastered the straight bits! I tied the piece of string, and used the spirit level thing, just like I watched you doing, but I've only managed to lay three bricks in all this time… and they're all wonky." I stood up and rubbed my back. "Oooh, that twinges!"

"I'll tell you what, Laura," he said, stifling a giggle and putting an arm around me. "You've clearly worn yourself out – I know how stiff a back can get with all that hard work – and there's not much prospect of either of us feeling like cooking. You get inside and have a nice hot bath, and I'll order us a takeaway."

He gave me a loving squeeze and a lopsided wink that I didn't really feel I deserved. "There's still plenty of daylight left, and it's cooler now, too. I might even get it finished before we eat."

"But that rogue brick is still there!"

"Does it really matter, love? You probably won't even notice it once you get used to it. And with a few plants trailing over the edge…"

He was right, of course.

"But I'll knock the whole thing down brick by brick and start again if I have to," he said. "If that's what it takes to make you happy and stop you moaning…"

new plants at the same time."

"A tile… now, why didn't I think of that? Or maybe one of those little terracotta smiley faces, like a sun or a moon. Do you know the ones I mean? It would give the planter a bit of character and make it look… well, happy!"

Feeling suddenly much happier myself, I kissed him and handed him the trowel.

"Oh, and Steve…"

"Yes, love?"

"I was thinking that, while we're at the garden centre, maybe we could buy a barbecue. One of those round metal ones, on wheels. We could keep it in the garage

I saw the little glint of pleasure in his eyes at the thought of sizzling coals

"I'm sorry. I have been moaning a bit today, haven't I?"

"A bit? You could win gold medals for it!" He laughed. "Come here, you daft thing!" and he kissed me on the end of my nose, which was feeling decidedly burned from too much sitting in the sun.

Then we stood together for a moment, our hands entwined, just looking at the planter and its one tiny mistake.

"You know, love, it may not be exactly as you'd like it," he said. "But it'd be easy enough to patch up. We could cover that brick with a decorative tile or something. I bet they've got some nice ones down at the garden centre. We could go next weekend, and you can start choosing your

and get it out on sunny days. Maybe invite a few friends around for a burger, and to admire the garden. What do you think?"

"Good idea, love," he said, turning his back to me, but not before I saw the little glint of pleasure in his eyes at the thought of those sizzling coals and a pair of tongs in his hand…

He picked up another brick, knelt on the blanket on the grass, and set to work.

Arguments – who needs them? They just tear everything apart and leave you struggling to build it all back up again, brick by brick. Just like the planter, sometimes all a marriage needs is a little patching up, plenty of love, and a smiley face or two to make it perfect again.

THE AUTHOR SAYS… "I live with a partner who is good at DIY while I do most of the cooking and gardening. I wondered what problems we might have if we were to try reversing the roles."

Never Too Old!

Finding the prize conker apparently gave Lizzie considerable power over this nice, if eccentric, stranger

By Sarah Swatridge

L izzie stood up with the large horse chestnut in her hand. She was aware of the autumn sun on her back, and the feeling that someone was watching her.

"I'll have it, if you don't want it," said a male voice breaking into her thoughts and making her jump.

"Actually, I do. It's beautiful," said Lizzie as she admired the shiny conker in the palm of her hand.

"It's a whopper!" said Graham moving closer. "Do you play conkers?"

"No!" Lizzie laughed. "It must be forty years since I did, and then my brother always beat me."

"Look at the size of it." Graham held out a bag full of medium-sized conkers for her to compare.

"Aren't you a bit old to be playing conkers?" teased Lizzie.

"You're never too old for a bit of fun," replied Graham with a smile. "But actually they're for my grandchildren." He looked wistful for a moment. "Alfie's seven and Eve's three. I can't believe it really, how the time's gone. I've never actually met them, although I've seen loads of photos and I've talked to them on the computer – you know, on Skype."

"Do they live far away?" asked Lizzie.

"New Zealand. But they're coming to visit me next week and I want to give them a great time. I want to show them

"You're never too old for a bit of fun. Actually, they're for my grandchildren"

"I'll have it if you don't want it," repeated Graham. This time he reached out hopefully towards the prize conker, still in Lizzie's warm hand.

She looked down at it and then up at him. He had nice eyes and a friendly face.

"Why this one in particular?" she asked.

good old Britain at its best – possibly an old-fashioned, rose-tinted picture of Britain, but all the best bits, nonetheless."

"Like when we were kids…" Lizzie was feeling as though she'd known Graham all her life. "Long, sunny days. Playing in the **Continued overleaf**

park with friends, and not coming home until you're hungry. And then having good, hearty old-fashioned meals like shepherd's pie or lamb stew – followed by tinned peaches with Carnation milk."

"Now you're making me hungry!" Graham groaned. "But that's exactly what I mean." He paused for a moment, looking more serious. "Don't get me wrong, I love a pizza sometimes or to watch a DVD – but I want to be the sort of Grandpa that builds tree houses and…"

"Plays conkers?" finished Lizzie, handing over the giant conker. "Your need is greater than mine."

"If you don't play, why are you collecting them?"

"I live in the bungalow with the large garden on the high street. I spread them around the house to keep the spiders away."

"That's just an old wives' tale!" Graham snorted in amusement.

number. "Keep it handy – just in case the conkers ever let you down."

"Thank you," said Lizzie, accepting the card. "Actually, I'm really glad you've called round because I've got something for you. Come in."

She led him into her little kitchen at the back of the house.

"Look!" she exclaimed in triumph, and handed over a mammoth conker.

"Where on earth did you find this?"

"Near the doctor's surgery." Lizzie paused a moment as she looked at her guest. "You can have it – on one condition," she blurted out.

"What's that?" he asked, looking into her eyes. Yes, he did have kind eyes and a gentle face. Since they'd met on Thursday, she'd been unable to get him out of her mind and so she'd done a little research.

Retired and widowed just like her, she'd found out – and he lived in a cottage on the outskirts of the village.

"I got carried away," admitted Lizzie. "I forgot how much I enjoyed baking…"

"It works for me," replied Lizzie, perhaps a little too sharply. Embarrassed, she picked up her little bag of conkers and made her way home.

She was surprised the next day to find Graham standing on her doorstep.

"Sorry if I offended you," he said. "Just because I don't mind spiders, I should realise that not everyone likes them."

Lizzie shuddered. "I hate even the thought of them."

"I bought you this," said Graham, holding out a handmade business card. It had a picture of Spiderman and his phone

"You use up your windfalls," she told him. "They're just wasted, lying around on the grass in your garden."

He raised an eyebrow at this display of inside information.

"Well, I'm not much of a cook. Carole did all that sort of thing."

"Well if you collect them up, I'd be happy to do some baking and split them half and half."

"Deal," said Graham quickly. "I'll go right home and collect them up now."

He was as good as his word, and was back to deliver several bucketfuls of apples later that same afternoon.

"I'll never eat all those!" Graham told her the following day when he called in to invite her out for a coffee. Lizzie laughed.

"I've done these small ones for you and I to put in the freezer. This large apple and blackberry pie is for when your family come over from New Zealand."

"Oh, they'll love that," said Graham enthusiastically. "And what's that?"

"I got carried away," admitted Lizzie. "I'd forgotten how much I enjoyed baking, and I've made a cake and some biscuits."

"I called in to invite you out for a coffee, but…"

Lizzie smiled and flicked the kettle on.

"Have tea and cake with me today and perhaps we could go for a coffee tomorrow?"

"Hmmm. Sounds like a date?" said Graham quietly, meeting her eye.

"A date with Spiderman!" mused Lizzie. "I wonder what my grandchildren would say about that?"

"Is that a problem?" asked Graham, looking suddenly anxious.

"Well – there is one condition," began Lizzie solemnly.

Graham nodded. "I had a feeling there might be. Go on."

"You must leave the skin-tight Spiderman outfit at home!" Lizzie told him, trying not to laugh.

"Ah. No problem." Graham grinned in relief. "Although I might have one condition, too."

"And what would that be?" asked Lizzie with a mischievous smile.

"We'll need to brush up on our conker skills. We can't have the grandchildren beating us all the time."

"I'm up for a challenge," agreed Lizzie.

Graham cut the cake while she made the tea. He wore a grin reminiscent of a Cheshire Cat, and Lizzie wondered if maybe he would turn out to be her conkering hero in more ways than one.

THE AUTHOR SAYS… "I love autumn, not only for the changing colours, but the diamond-like spider's webs and the crispness in the air. I love collecting blackberries and, of course, playing conkers!"

ILLUSTRATIONS: MANDY DIXON, SHUTTERSTOCK

Izzie's Tree

Deep in Epping Forest in the golden days of the early 70s, three children were growing up happy and free

By Barbara Featherstone

We called it the Upper. It was our own special tree, but we always quarrelled over its name.

"It's Izzie's Tree," declared Izzie. "I saw it first!"

She stared at Johnny and me, her gaze darting from one to the other, her blue eyes glinting with easy tears. There was a swing to her fat blonde plaits, a pout of the buttoned lips. Her freckles stood out like orange sultanas. Johnny was always teasing her about those freckles.

Izzie was the youngest. Johnny and I

we found our special tree. We were out playing in Epping Forest. We played there every Saturday; Johnny, Izzie and me. We played out in sun, rain and snow. Providing the sun wasn't too hot, the rain too heavy, or the snow too deep.

The Forest fringed the unmade road where we three kids lived, just a few doors apart. I loved that road. Cows would appear, on hot summer afternoons, as if from nowhere. They were big, bony cows. Black and white cows. Their satiny hides silky-shivering. Their beautiful eyes soft-staring. Long lashes blinking the flies away, tails flicking. They would amble

We always felt safe. Friends and neighbours looked out for each other

were eleven, tall and skinny. But Izzie was only eight, plump and short. She was so easy to tease, and sometimes I joined in. Though Johnny and I never went too far – and we always looked out for each other. Especially Izzie.

"It's Izzie's Tree," Izzie said again, and stamped her foot. Tears and tantrums were her only defence. Though neither lasted long. Moments later, she would be full of smiles and happiness and sunshine; our little quarrels forgotten.

It was a Saturday, I remember, when

carelessly along our dry, dusty road, swiping mouthfuls of neighbours' hedges.

Sometimes, in the sleepy haze of a warm summer's afternoon, a garden gate might be left carelessly unlatched. Then the huge black and white cows would thrust forward. Greedy for the cool green grass, their great lolloping tongues pink-licking.

There were no lamp posts down our road. Not then. At night, the street lay hushed in silence, cocooned in darkness. Going to the local cinema with Mum some

evenings, negotiating the roughened ground, was an adventure. Or coming home from school on dusky winter afternoons, but we were always together.

Yet we always felt safe. There were friends and neighbours to look out for each other. Like Johnny and I looked out for Izzie when playing out in the forest.

Christmas was magic. It was the only time when we three kids were allowed out on our own in the dark. Even then, we **Continued overleaf** went as soon as the first stars pricked faintly, and we were restricted to just our road, only, where we were known.

Johnny, Izzie and I wandered up and down our road like the cows, our way faint-lit by curtained windows; a sliver of yellow light sometimes slicing through.

The night air was bitter-sharp, stars like scraps of silver foil, so close you felt you could reach out and touch them.

We sang carols in the chill comfort of the dark. We sang all the favourite carols. *Away in a Manger, Once in Royal David's City*, and *Oh, Little Town of Bethlehem*.

When we finished, we'd knock on the door, stand there on the doorstep, tingling with anticipation; our breath misting the cold air like dandelion puffballs.

Sometimes, we were asked to sing another verse, another carol or two. Often, we were welcomed inside by a kind neighbour and given lemonade, a hot mince pie, and a handful of copper coins.

bedtime. We climbed trees; jumped streams; bought fizzy lemon and raspberry-flavoured sherbet, liquorice and ice lollies from the Green Man – a small wooden kiosk deep in the trees.

We made dams, fished for tiddlers, and slip-slid across the lake when it froze over. We were home by sunset in summer, dusk in winter. If we were wanted, Johnny's father would come to the edge of the Forest; his voice hoarse and reaching, like a foghorn across the sea. "Joh…nny…!"

We knew all the trees in the Forest; the oak, the holly, the beech, the hawthorn with those fascinating little wavy leaves which we kids nibbled and called "bread and cheese". Our special find was a young oak. A forked branch angled low, just within our reach, its supple bendiness enticing.

"I saw the tree first," said Izzie, lips still pouting, cheeks shiny pink. "I want to call it Izzie's Tree."

I felt a strange tingle. Perhaps it was

Izzie was the best climber. She was up the tree like a squirrel, confident and agile

With the modest offerings, we three children would buy Christmas presents for our friends and family.

Winter times were special times; the trees in the Forest frost-sparkling; damp-dark leaves and twigs snapping underfoot, but the hours were short for playing out. Summer time in Epping Forest was our favourite.

We spent whole days in the Forest on Saturdays; me, Johnny and Izzie. Sundays were family days. Weekdays we snatched the hours between after homework and

some kind of premonition. There was something different about Izzie today. It wasn't like her to hold out this long.

Johnny stepped forward into the crook of the fork, looping an arm over each branch; testing his weight. He drew in his breath and jumped, springing higher and higher. He stopped, out of breath, cheeks flushed.

"My go now," said Izzie, pushing forward.

Johnny shook his head. "It's Vee's go next. You're the baby, Izzie. You go last."

He gazed up at the tree, still breathing

hard. "The Upper's a good name."

"It's Izzie's Tree!" She scowled round at me, daring me.

There were scarlet bows on the ends of Izzie's plaits, primped like two starched butterflies. My plaits were scrunched with rubber bands.

My glance slid from hers. I shrugged. And the name was decided. The Upper.

I had my turn then. At first it was thrilling, my heart leaping with every spring of the branches. Then I saw the look on Izzie's face.

"It's your go now," I told her.

She was too small to reach the crook, so Johnny lifted her up. She curled her arms over the bendy branches and gave delicious little screams as Johnny and I pumped the branches up and down.

When the three of us got tired of jumping, we climbed the Upper. This time we let Izzie go first. Though rounded with baby fat, Izzie was the best climber. She was up the trees like a squirrel, confident

and agile, and often climbed much higher than Johnny and me.

Izzie was up the Upper a long time. I stared up at her through the patchwork branches. She was wearing a red sticky-out dress that day. I thought she was like an angel on a Christmas tree with that dress and her gold hair.

"I can see you knickers," chanted Johnny. "They're navy blue."

They were Izzie's school knickers, same as all us girls wore. Droopy, with a pocket for a hanky. The elastic waist never tight enough. We were always hitching at them.

Johnny began to tramp impatiently about the tree. Dry twigs and decaying acorns crackled into the silence as he scuffed at the ground, the soil that dark-rich glisten of black treacle.

"What are you doing up there, Izzie?"

Her voice drifted down to us with a scattering of leaves.

"I can see Heaven, Johnny. The sky's this beautiful blue. There's lots of angels. They've got these big floaty wings, and I can hear lovely singing."

Johnny grinned at me.

On Monday, Izzie wasn't at the Forest when Johnny and I arrived. We waited for her by the Upper, taking it in turns to let the bendy branches carry us higher and higher as we sprang.

Izzie wasn't poorly. She'd been to school. The three of us walked together every morning. I'd seen her later in the playground too, and we'd all walked home together.

After a bit, Johnny and I got tired of the waiting. We called Izzie's name again and again but there was no answer. So we
Continued overleaf

Continued from previous page

tugged off our shoes and socks, tucked the socks into our pockets, tied our laces together and strung our shoes around our necks. Then we padded in the stream.

There were only certain places we three went. Only certain places we met up. We always knew how to find each other. Yet by sunset, Izzie still hadn't come.

A while later, we heard Johnny's dad through the trees, "Joh…nny…!"

On our way back home we passed by the Upper. As we drew close to our special tree, the Forest darkened; a velvety blackness that swooped without warning. I clutched at Johnny's sleeve and we stood there, staring.

The only light came from the Upper. The tree blazed a dazzling white, a shine of gold glinting through the topmost branches. Like an angel with a halo. And I thought then of Izzie.

Then the strange light was changing; misting into rose, into purple, into lilac and into lavender; the colours coming and going.

I heard Johnny's breath sizzle through his teeth. "There's this word, Vee…

"What word, Johnny?"

"Soul."

There was the shake of tears in his voice. "Is this is it, Vee? Is this someone's… soul…?"

I couldn't answer. And then, suddenly, the Forest was itself again; the smoke-blue fade of day, the raw-sweet smell of the Forest floor, birds singing, and the green gold of the leaves. Johnny started to run. Then he stopped and darted back. He grabbed at my hand, and we ran together.

At home, nothing was said. Children lived in bubbles then. Cosy, safe bubbles called childhood. But I eavesdropped when our big black phone rang, and I shivered because I was afraid of that monster.

My father answered it. I heard him say, "I'm so sorry, Charlie…," and my father's voice was deep and low and mournful like the chimes of our grandfather clock.

Charlie was Izzie's dad.

Next day was Tuesday. After homework, I skipped out to play with Johnny in the Forest. We made a bridge of stepping stones across the stream.

I hopped from stone to stone, glancing back over my shoulder, telling Johnny in snatches all about my dad talking to Izzie's dad, Charlie, on our big black monster phone.

Johnny followed me across the stream. He slipped once, just before he got to the bank, and got mud all over his knobbly bare knees.

He jumped up, laughing. Then his bright laughter faded.

"I saw Izzie's mum when I was coming to the Forest."

I stared round at him. "Did you say about Izzie?"

He nodded. "Yes. I said, was Izzie

coming to the Forest today?"

"And what did she say?"

"Nothing. She just shook her head and walked away." Johnny sleeved his nose.

"She looked really sad, Vee. Her face was all white. You know, like the chalk at school. And she had all these crinkly lines that went right across her forehead."

We started walking towards the Green Man. I had pocket money for sherbet.

Johnny kicked up a cloud of leaves.

"I think something bad has happened to Izzie." He swiped a trickle of mud from of coats, satchels and plimsoll bags.

When I got home from school that day, I heard our phone start ringing. Dad was at work, so Mum had to answer. She walked up the hall in slow steps, stopped by the phone and stared down at it. She picked up the receiver, holding it gingerly between her thumb and forefinger as if it might come alive and bite her. Like me, she was afraid of that big black monster.

Mum didn't say much on the phone, just "yes" and "no", and once "oh,

She walked up the hall in slow steps, stopped and stared down at the phone

his knee. "Do you think she's dead, Vee? Do you think that was Izzie's soul we saw by the Upper?"

I watched the cloud of leaves settle, breathing in the sweet-sharp scent of the Forest. I didn't know what to think.

All I could see in my mind's eye were Izzie's orange sultana freckles, and I remembered how Johnny was always teasing her about them.

It was three days before Johnny and I found out what happened to Izzie that Monday.

My teacher, Miss Harrison, found me crying one playtime. I was huddled up on the wooden bench in the cloakroom, hiding my distress behind the musty hang really?", in her special telephone voice, and just at the end, of course "goodbye", and "thank you for calling".

Then Mum and I went into the kitchen. Mum made a pot of tea, and jam on toast. She said it was my teacher who had telephoned. The teacher had told Mum all about finding me crying in the cloakroom. Mum asked, was I upset about Izzie? Was I crying because Izzie had been knocked down by a lorry?

I said I didn't know about Izzie being knocked down by a lorry.

Then Mum put her arms about me. She explained gently, her voice soft and quiet.

On Monday, Izzie had been on an errand after school. She was racing fast to

Continued overleaf

Continued from previous page

get the errand done because she was meeting Johnny and me in the Forest later. There was a small side road to cross.

Izzie had forgotten the new Green Cross Code, drummed into us daily both at home and at school. STOP, LOOK AND LISTEN. She didn't see the lorry as it came swinging round the corner.

The ambulance took Izzie to hospital. Izzie was very poorly. Her mum and dad visited every day. Izzie had nearly died, but the doctors and nurses had saved her.

Mum held me tight. She said Izzie would have to stay in hospital for quite a long time, but she was a strong little girl and one day she would be well again.

An hour in the Forest might do her good. But we were to take extra care of her

Though Izzie, said Mum, would never be quite the same Izzie as before.

Mum was right. When Izzie came home, she was changed. She'd grown taller somehow. Her baby fat was gone. She didn't wear short sticky-out dresses any more. Her hems hung below her knees. She was like a doll left out in the rain, her brightness gone.

The orange freckles were faded to a dusty gold. She walked with a twisty leg.

Johnny and I called round for her one time. Johnny said to Izzie's mum, could we take Izzie to the Forest?

Izzie's mum said she didn't know about that, but Izzie's dad, Charlie, said why not? Izzie hadn't been out for a while. She wasn't even back at school yet. An hour or so, he said, might do her good, but Johnny and I were to be careful. We were to take extra special care of Izzie.

We went to our special tree. We didn't do climbing, but Johnny and I pumped the bendy branches while Izzie jumped on one foot. She could do a whole minute.

I watched her fingers trail the rough bark of the tree.

"Izzie's Tree," said Johnny.

And Izzie smiled.

THE AUTHOR SAYS... "My London childhood was idyllic. Climbing trees in Epping Forest, making dams, fishing – just being. That lovely freedom. Our special tree, the Upper."

Berry Butterfly Cakes

Ingredients (Makes 12)

- ✦ **100g butter, softened**
- ✦ **100g caster sugar**
- ✦ **2 medium eggs, beaten**
- ✦ **½tsp vanilla extract**
- ✦ **100g self-raising flour**
- ✦ **Pinch of salt**

To decorate:

- ✦ **75g butter, softened**
- ✦ **150g icing sugar, plus extra for sprinkling**
- ✦ **½tsp vanilla extract**
- ✦ **4tbsp strawberry or raspberry jam**
- ✦ **6 strawberries, sliced**
- ✦ **12 raspberries**

1 Preheat the oven to 180°C, fan oven 160°C, Gas Mark 4. Place 12 paper bun cases into a bun tray.

2 Beat the butter and sugar together until pale and creamy, using a wooden spoon or hand-held electric whisk. Gradually beat in the eggs, then stir in the vanilla.

3 Sift in the flour and salt, folding in gently with a large metal spoon. Spoon into the bun cases. Bake towards the centre of the oven for 18-20min until risen and golden. Cool completely.

4 For the filling, beat the butter until creamy, then beat in the icing sugar and vanilla. Cut the tops off the buns and slice in two to make "wings". Place 1tsp jam into each bun, then pipe or spoon the buttercream on top. Position the wings in place, with strawberry slices on top. Pop the raspberries in the centre and sprinkle with icing sugar.

RECIPE AND FOOD STYLING: SUE ASHWORTH PHOTOGRAPHY: JONATHAN SHORT

At The Four Feathers

The storm had thrown them together in this out-of-the-way hostelry – and Mary sensed something was amiss

By Anna Eliot

I t was a dark and stormy night, the kind that kept sensible folk within doors by the fireside. Drenching rain was flung against the casements of the thatched Four Feathers inn by a driving wind that threatened to rip leaves from their branches long before their traditional autumn shedding.

Mary Treeves shivered, fastened the window latch of the best guest bedroom then took a final look round at her preparations. Satisfied, she collected up her newly-stripped linen and hurried back was drifting through from the taproom. Balancing her linen bundle on one hip, Mary eased open the oak door to peep within. Behind the bar, her benevolent father Albert Treeves was assiduously cleaning glasses, with one eye on the group gathered round the glowing hearth.

They were an odd assembly, as any strangers thrown together by mischance were likely to be. To Mary, endlessly fascinated by folk in all their forms, they were unexpected fodder for her underfed imagination.

Thanks to a post-chaise accident, the richly-apparelled Lady Almeria Buxton

Her sympathy for the chaperone was soon transferred to the orphaned maid

down the steep main stairway and into the flagstoned corridor linking the warren of upper floors, taproom and kitchen.

She should not frown upon the weather, for it had brought the inn some much-needed custom by forcing travellers to seek shelter in a house that all too often these days was passed by for larger, more conveniently placed establishments.

The sound of a deep storyteller's voice had sought refuge at the Feathers, along with her ungracious nephew who'd made no secret of his displeasure in having to stay in such a poky house.

"Oh, do stop whining, Egerton," Lady Almeria commanded as she bent to push a plumed monstrosity of a hat – now sadly bedraggled –through the doorway. "This place is dry and clean, and **Continued overleaf**

The Feathers was
clean and welcoming
if not luxurious

Continued from previous page

something smells quite delicious…"

"That's my daughter's chicken broth, the best in the shire," said Alfred proudly.

"We will have two bowls, then," Egerton grunted, shrugging off his dripping cloak and shoving it at the landlord, "and your two best rooms for the Lady Almeria and myself."

Then there was the young merchant's ward and her companion, supposedly interrupting their journey on account of the elder's rheumatism, so painful in wet weather, though Mary suspected that Miss Louisa Dove had seized the opportunity for possible adventure before being respectably confined to a Bath seminary.

Mary's initial pity for the chaperone in having an impetuous charge like Miss Dove was soon transferred to the orphaned maid. With such a sour-puss for companion, how had the pretty thing managed to remain so upbeat?

The storyteller, a pedlar of some sort, sat on a stool close to the fire, where the flames danced a waltz across his weather-beaten face. He would have been tall if not for the hunch in his shoulders, but his voice made up for his lack of physical presence. From his opening words of, "It was on just such a night as this, and in much the same style of inn, that a man lost his mind…", and then on through his tale of a traveller forced to shelter at a deserted inn deep in the forest, he'd held the attention of his audience – even the sulky Egerton, who'd originally attempted to banish the man from the fireside, as if his very presence in some way contaminated the finer gentleman.

"Not so hasty, sir," the pedlar had cautioned with an enigmatic smile. "I have treasures in this here chest."

"Ignore my nephew," Lady Almeria instructed as she sank her ample figure into the largest available chair and gazed eagerly at the pedlar's basket by his rough-shod feet. "Have you any ribbons or plumage amongst your wares?"

"All that and more," promised the pedlar, drawing an excited squeal from Miss Dove before she'd plunged her hands into the basket.

Her scowling chaperone was itching to whisk the girl away from such an influence. Mary could sympathise to a certain extent. There was something about the wanderer. Even her father, an easy-going host as a rule, had only offered him a bed in the stables, as if he didn't trust him in the main house.

Miss Dove was begging him to continue with his story.

"So what did the man see when he relit his candle?"

"He could see a hole dug out of the cellar floor," the pedlar said in a smoky voice, "and something moving inside, writhing like an angry snake but making no sound. A cold finger of fear shot down his spine. He turned to leave, but the door was shut fast. He looked back, trembling now, as the shadow rose up off the floor. It was completely covered by a heavy, worm-ridden shroud; a death shroud.

"'Get back!' the man cried, brandishing his candle like a priest with his cross as the figure turned and began floating toward him. The man had just realised it had no feet when it dragged the veil from its head and where a face should have been, was naught but a gaping hole…"

Miss Dove uttered a shriek, a small hand flying to her throat.

Egerton snorted.

"Pay no heed, Miss. Ghosts do not exist."

The pedlar tapped the side of his head, smiling mysteriously.

"So some say. But whatever happened at that lonely inn, our hero's hair turned pure white overnight. He was never the same again."

Miss Dove's delicious shudder was

"I doubt it, in a place like this," grunted Egerton, taking the candlestick Mary proffered without even a glance at her.

Mary glared at his retreating form. The Four Feathers may not be luxurious, but it was cosy, warm and spotlessly clean. And it was home. She didn't appreciate it being scorned so unjustly.

Turning away, she caught the pedlar watching her.

"Good night, miss," he murmured, doffing his threadbare cap as he shuffled off towards the stables. "Sleep tight, now."

She watched, frowning, until he disappeared. It was probably just fancy, brought about by the turbulent night and the spooky web the wanderer had woven, but she had an uneasy feeling. One that overshadowed the old, familiar comfort of the Feathers and had her checking shadows for unwelcome strangers, living or otherwise…

Out in the yard the storm whipped her hair, then killed her candle flame

spoiled by her companion roughly seizing her elbow.

"Enough tales. It's past your bedtime."

Albert Treeves came out from behind the bar, fat candle in hand.

"I'll show you upstairs. It's a wild night out there, for sure, but you're safe here inside The Feathers, miss. There's no ghosts or draughts here. You'll sleep snug in your beds."

And he escorted the pair – one disapproving, one extremely disappointed – out of the room.

"Fetch a light, Egerton," Lady Almeria ordered, heaving herself out of the chair. "I want my bed."

Some time later, in her tiny bedroom under the eaves, Mary abandoned all efforts to sleep. She was still tormented by that niggling suspicion of danger. Arming herself with a poker and a flickering candle flame, she slipped from her room and down the sloping steps of the old Tudor floor onto the main landing.

All was quiet and yet, she sensed, not quite still. Her mind flew to the pedlar. She crept downstairs and out into the yard.

The tail end of the storm whipped her hair into her face, then killed her candle flame. She stumbled to the stables and paused on the threshold. Before her eyes

Continued overleaf

across the yard and Mary noticed, as his lithe frame filled the kitchen doorway, that his hunchback had completely disappeared.

They stood pressed against the stairwell for what seemed an age, Mary's nerves tight as bowstrings as the silence stretched on. Then she heard shuffled movement and glimpsed a shadowy figure creeping along the passage.

The pedlar pulled her close, his words little more than a sigh across her cheek as he whispered, "Back stairs."

When the door to the best guest bedroom began to inch open, he added, "Go," and pushed her gently away.

Continued from previous page

had adjusted to the darkness, she was grabbed from behind and a hand covered her mouth, cutting off the shocked gasp in her throat.

"I won't hurt you," the pedlar's voice breathed in her ear. "But you mustn't scream. Understand?"

When Mary nodded, the hand was removed.

"Why are you out of bed, little lady?"

"I sensed something amiss," Mary whispered back. "So I came to investigate."

The thieves never knew how such an ungainly man as the pedlar could have come upon them unawares. But just as they were preparing to depart the scene of their latest crime, he burst into the room, his shouts enough to wake the dead, let alone the landlord of this rat's-nest.

One broke free from the maelstrom he'd created in Lady Buxton's bedroom to

He hesitated, then reached for her hand and seemed about to speak

She heard the whisper of a laugh.

"Why am I not surprised?" He took hold of her chin, turning her toward him. "I don't have much time, so I must ask you to trust me. Can you do that?"

Mary found herself nodding.

"Good girl. What is that, a poker? Keep hold of it; it may be useful. Now, come with me and stay silent."

Taking her hand, he led her swiftly

slip into the passage and along to the back stairs, where freedom beckoned… blocked by the landlord's resolute daughter.

"Going somewhere, Miss Dove?"

The maid's face twisted in an ugly snarl before she launched herself at Mary, spitting and clawing. Mary was more than a match for her, though. She'd not lived at an inn for all of her nineteen years without learning a move or two.

Dawn was breaking when the pedlar once more sat before a blazing hearth and told a tale, this time just for the landlord's daughter.

"My name is Thomas North. I'm from the Bow Street justice league, and we've been tracking this mother-and-daughter criminal act south of the Thames ever since London got too hot for them. They've been preying on rich travellers in coaching inns – even killed a man who saw too much one night."

Recalling "Miss Dove's" engaging artlessness, Mary shivered.

"I truly believed she was somebody's ward on her way to Bath – even pitied her," she muttered.

"So did everyone who met them. Their disguise was very good."

"As was yours," Mary scolded softly, meeting the Runner's eyes for the first time since his revelation.

Thomas North hesitated, then reached for her hand. He was about to speak when Mary's father came in from the yard.

"Cart's all ready, and the criminals secured, sir."

North nodded his thanks.

"Then I'll be on my way."

Yawning, Treeves collapsed before the fireside for an extra hour's snooze before the Feathers shook itself awake for a new day.

Mary followed North to the door where he looked her over, an admiring gleam in his eye.

"You're wasted at this inn, you know, with those instincts of yours," he said finally. "Not to mention that right hook…"

Mary smiled.

"Perhaps. But this is home, and Father needs me."

North nodded, his answering smile sympathetic if rather sad.

"Then fare you well, Mary Treeves, until another storm blows me back along this way."

And he bent and stole a kiss before heading round to the yard, where the two tricksters were trussed and waiting for his escort.

Mary leaned against the door frame, listening for the sound of cart wheels above the creak of the inn sign. Thieves and cut-throats at the Four Feathers! A legitimate reason, perhaps, for the patronising Egerton not to settle his bill, though it would be with Lady Almeria's money either way.

She watched horse and cart clip-clop past on its way to London, seeing not the thieves in the back but the Bow Street Runner's broad shoulders and confident hands on the reins, until he was swallowed up by the morning mist.

Someone had stolen something from the inn after all, she realised, pressing her fingers to her quivering mouth. But this particular thief would be welcomed back with open arms whenever he chanced to venture this way again.

She was already greatly looking forward to that day…

THE AUTHOR SAYS… "A winter's night in Suffolk at a pub with a creaking sign, and thoughts of highwaymen dancing round my head, was the spark for this story!"

I Will Fear Nothing

She had no choice, she was to be married – yet Aline had a burning curiosity she wished to satisfy first…

By Angela Pickering

T he sounds and smells of the tourney almost overwhelmed Aline de Bressant as she slipped unnoticed from her tent.

She could hear the clash of metal as the young squires prepared the knights' swords and armour and the creaking of the leather harnesses on the destriers, the great war-horses. Then there was the stamping sound of their iron-shod hooves and their snorting breath as they waited, already clothed in their own armour for the battle to come.

Aline wrinkled her nose at the stench of the sweat of horses and men and trembled under the onrush of sensations,

This was the first time Aline had been allowed to attend one of the mock battles that her father, William de Bressant, followed through the season. They took place throughout the summer at different venues across the country.

Aline's mother often travelled too, making quite considerable sums of money by wagering on her chosen knight of the day… who was not always her husband.

Aline almost darted back inside, but the flapping of the emblazoned De Bressant standard on top of her tent seemed to reproach her. The De Bressant coat of arms that her father would shortly carry into battle made her lift her head and square her slight shoulders.

"I am a De Bressant," she muttered

She almost darted back inside, but the emblazoned flag seemed to reproach her

which were as nothing compared to the excitement that charged the air. The tourney, although considered sport, was almost as good as war itself to these hardened knights, and sometimes every bit as dangerous.

under her breath. "Fear Nothing."

The family motto had never seemed so appropriate as at this moment when she was about to embark upon this, her first independent adventure. Taking a huge
Continued overleaf

After the summer tourney she was to be wed

breath, Aline slipped away from the tents and pavilions of her family.

The ground underfoot was already churned into a muddy swamp by horses' hooves and booted feet and Aline had to lift her trailing skirts from the mud as she walked. She blessed the foresight that had made her borrow her maid, Belle's, clothing before setting out.

No one would spare a glance at a lowly maid running an errand or placing a wager for her mistress, and Belle was sworn to secrecy as she waited, dressed only in her chemise, in the tent they shared.

Weaving her way through the gaily-coloured tents, Aline kept her courage by reciting to herself the names of the knights whose pennants flew from the pavilions. Part of her education as the daughter of a knight of the realm had been to study the meaning of the emblems and colours.

At last she recognised the arms of Sir Henry Glennister, who was reputedly one of the most skilful knights among the English contingent. Aline shuddered at the thought that the cold, austere island across the sea would soon be her new home. Glennister was the knight to whom Aline was to be married within a few short days.

"I cannot marry a man whom I have never seen," she had protested to her mother some weeks earlier, when she had first been told of her father's plans for her.

"It is not my decision, Aline," replied her mother, seemingly unmoved. "You are a young woman now, and 'tis past time you were wed."

"But, Mother…"

The conversation had been cut short by the arrival of De Bressant himself and no more could be said. All Aline knew was that she was to go to Glennister as his wife after the tourney in the summer.

She peered from behind the flaps of a wine-coloured pavilion and watched the antics of Glennister's two squires as they prepared their master for the mock battle. She had sworn a solemn oath to herself that she would not marry any man sight-unseen and this was the purpose of her secret expedition. She had no intention of being presented to her future bridegroom without knowing anything at all about him.

She devoured the tall figure with her eyes: the dull metal links that seemed to cover his whole body, the greying hair that spilled to his shoulders.

Grey hair? she thought with horror, and her heart leapt into her throat. *They are giving me to an old man.*

Through the tears that suddenly pricked at her eyes, she watched, aghast, as Glennister turned her way. She saw his face and stifled a cry of dismay with her hand. He was indeed old, and even from a distance, Aline could see the terrible scar that ran from temple to chin. It looked as though some enemy had hewn Sir Henry's face in half.

One of the knight's attendants handed him a cup of wine and Aline saw the distorted smile he bestowed on the young man. She licked her lips as she watched the knight sipping the wine; her own mouth suddenly as parched as the dried fruit with which she had broken her fast that morning.

She wished briefly that she had been born a man who could take the cross and defy fate by fighting for God in the Holy Land. She was unaware of the warmth of

"I shall buy you a new gown," Aline promised as Belle wiped her mistress' hot and tear-stained face. She shuddered. "After I am married."

"Are you prepared, Aline?" The flap of the tent opened and her mother entered. "Leave us," she ordered, casting a puzzled glance at Belle's muddied hem. "I shall help Aline now."

Once they were alone together Clare de Bressant smiled at her daughter and, taking up her tortoiseshell comb, began to dress her hair.

"Your hair is your best feature," she remarked, running the comb through the silken threads. "The Glennisters are fortunate indeed to have De Bressant blood to mix with their own."

She smiled. Her heart may be dead in her chest but she knew wherein lay her duty

the tears that now ran freely down her cheeks as she compared the appealing face of the young squire with that of his aged master. The ravaged face and wispy hair could only suffer from the contrast with the youth's clear skin and dark locks.

At last Aline wiped her face with her sleeve. She knew that such thoughts ill became a young lady of her status. Mud splattered her maid's skirts and coated her feet and ankles as she ran through the mire back to the De Bressant tents.

"I saw him," she told her relieved maid, and remembering his smile, added, "He looked kind."

Belle was too busy bathing Aline's grimy feet to ask any questions. She was none too pleased with the state of her gown after Aline's excursion and made her feelings quite clear.

Aline was soon dressed in a blue silk gown, with a silver belt slung around her hips. Her golden braids hung to her waist and were covered by a shimmering gauze veil topped with a circlet of silver.

"There," said her mother, standing back to admire the full effect. "Fear Nothing, Aline De Bressant."

Aline lifted her head and smiled at her mother. Her heart may well be broken and dead in her chest, but she knew wherein lay her duty. She was, after all, her father's daughter and could not, in reality, escape to go crusading.

She smiled again as she imagined herself dressed in boy's clothes with a cross on her tunic. She could barely lift her father's sword, and had once been severely punished for trying

Continued overleaf

Continued from previous page

Her little giggle at the thought caused her mother to look intently into her face. She gazed steadfastly back. There were other ways of showing courage than killing the infidel, she thought. She would not shame her family.

"Come," said Clare. "We need to give our favours to our knights before they go to do battle."

Aline had a blue silk scarf, matching her dress, for her betrothed to carry into mock warfare. This would be the first time she would see him, at least officially.

Although the tourney would range far and wide across the surrounding fields, the ladies were to watch parts of it from a

looking for the greying head of Sir Henry.

At last, as her father moved away, she saw him. He was accepting the favour of a portly lady in red some way up the field.

She frowned.

"Mother," she said, "why is Sir Henry accepting the favour of another lady? Is that not extremely ill-mannered, since I am here waiting to meet him?"

Clare was barely listening, her eyes following the knights and ladies surrounding them.

"That is not Henry Glennister, you silly goose," she murmured impatiently through the side of her mouth. "That's his father." She pulled Aline closer to her side. "Your own betrothed is approaching now.

"That is not Henry Glennister, you silly goose," Clare murmured impatiently

raised wooden platform. The knights would approach the ladies before battle to collect their favours to wear on the arm, the lance or the helm. Sometimes, if the lady were especially favoured, the knight would even tuck the token into his hauberk next to the heart. Aline wondered if, when the time came, she would care where Sir Henry carried her scarf.

Clare smiled at her husband as he lifted his visor and tied her own scarf to his arm. He spared a glance for his daughter, and nodded, as if pleased with what he saw. She cast anxious glances around the field through her lowered eyelashes,

Henry Glennister the younger." She lowered her head in a bow, still whispering to Aline. "He has been knighted only today. This is his first tourney too."

Aline sank into a graceful curtsey, her blue favour clutched in nerveless fingers.

"Fear Nothing," she muttered, as her eyes travelled up the armoured legs and body standing before her, and registered the jet black hair tumbling around broad youthful shoulders.

And bravely Aline De Bressant lifted her gaze until at last she was looking into the dark, smiling eyes of her handsome future husband.

THE AUTHOR SAYS... "I grew up on a diet of stories about knights and their ladies. The reality was certainly less attractive than Hollywood used to make it, but oh, oh, Ivanhoe."

Bonfire Cup Cakes

Ingredients (Makes 12)

- ✦ **110g butter**
- ✦ **110g light muscovado sugar**
- ✦ **110g black treacle**
- ✦ **175g plain flour**
- ✦ **Pinch of salt**
- ✦ **1tsp ground ginger**
- ✦ **1 large egg, beaten**
- ✦ **150ml milk**
- ✦ **1 level tsp baking powder**
  For The Topping:
- ✦ **100g butter**
- ✦ **200g icing sugar**
- ✦ **50g cinder toffee, chopped**
- ✦ **2 chocolate flake bars, broken up**

1 Preheat the oven to 190°C, fan oven 170°C, Gas Mark 5. Put 12 cup cake cases into a muffin tin.

2 Put the butter, sugar and black treacle into a saucepan and heat gently until melted. Don't allow the mixture to get too hot. Cool slightly.

3 Sift the flour, salt and ginger into a mixing bowl. Stir in the melted mixture and eggs. Warm the milk and add the baking powder, then stir into the bowl. Pour into a jug and share between the cake cases. Bake for 22-25min until risen and firm. Cool on a wire rack.

4 For the frosting, beat the butter and icing sugar together until light and creamy. Spread onto the cakes and top with cinder toffee and chocolate flake.

Cook's tip: Make 20 fairy cake-sized buns if you prefer, baking them for 20min.

RECIPE AND FOOD STYLING: SUE ASHWORTH PHOTOGRAPHY: JONATHAN SHORT

A Star Came Down

Beset by angels with flu, a leaky roof, a power cut and a crisis of confidence, how can the Nativity go ahead?

By Hayley Johnson-Mack

I 'm so sorry," Linda croaked down the phone into Sarah's ear. "I've caught the 'flu. You'll have to take over the directing the Nativity."

"Me?" Sarah gasped. "But I'm no drama teacher! I'm just your assistant."

"And you're brilliant at it, plus you've been at every rehearsal so you know the setup. Please, Sarah!"

Sarah swallowed. Ordinarily, she loved being involved with the atmospheric St Saviour's church, but never had the success of anything rested solely on her shoulders. Linda had arranged to stage a special Nativity to help raise funds for much-needed restoration work, and with a new young vicar with something to prove at the helm, Sarah knew how important the Christmas show was this year. She took a deep breath.

"I'll do my best," she promised.

Armed with Linda's files, an anxious Sarah arrived at the red-bricked rectory that afternoon.

The Rev Richard Harman was waiting with coffee and a cosy fire to keep out the December chill. Sarah's heart sank when she saw his face. Not because it wasn't nice to look at; in fact, she found it uncomfortably appealing. But it currently wore that gently sympathetic expression she'd seen at funerals.

"I'm afraid Linda's not the only one to get this bug," he explained.

Sarah's stomach lurched.

"Please tell me it isn't Jenny."

Jenny Lees was an extremely gifted eight-year-old with the singing voice of a nightingale. She was their star attraction; Linda had practically written the play around her talent.

"Not Jenny. But other angels, two shepherds – and the innkeeper."

Continued overleaf

His face wore that gently sympathetic expression she'd seen at funerals

Resisting the urge to plunge her head in her hands, Sarah scoured Linda's register for a potential new cast. It would need imagination but she could switch a few parts, recruit some neighbours... There had to be a way to save the show.

"I'll see what I can sort," she said aloud.

A strong hand rested on her shoulder.

"I'm here to help," Rev Harman assured her. "So whatever you need, just ask."

"A bit of divine intervention might be handy." Sarah resisted the urge to lay her cheek against that hand.

He smiled. "I'll see what I can do."

There was a storm that night, one that rattled windows and blew down branches. Not a night to be away from the fireside.

Yet the man found himself fleeing through unfamiliar territory, the tempest pursuing him as relentlessly as the men he'd double-crossed. Diving into a churchyard, he stumbled over graves, trying not to think of what slept beneath.

Then a surprising glimmer of welcome, – a candle arch in a church window. Sanctuary! Finding the door locked, the man went to work on the heavy padlock. Pretty easy for someone with his skills.

Inside, all was still. His panting breaths split the silence. The light illumined columned pews, celestial statues and a Nativity stable.

The stranger stopped before it,

unexpected childhood memories warming his bones. This place was having a strange effect on him, making him regret...

Still, he had a job to do. Withdrawing a package from under his coat, he slid a collar of tiny teardrops onto his palm. As his eyes alighted on the "stable" and its contents, he allowed himself to smile.

Sarah slept badly, haunted by dreams of Nativity posters slashed with Cancelled stickers, so was rather bleary-eyed when she arrived at the church for emergency rehearsals.

Then came the second hammer-blow.

"We're leaking," Harman announced and showed Sarah where the storm had torn a hole in the lower roof. "The water's shorted out the electricity supply, and the engineers can't guarantee we'll be back on in time for the play. Plus someone broke in last night – though nothing was stolen."

Sarah collapsed on the altar steps.

"I knew it!" She moaned. "I knew I'd not be good enough to save the play!"

Harman thrust a mug of steaming coffee into her hands then sat beside her.

"You see that display?" He pointed at the painted Bethlehem stable, a silver foil star shining atop the panelled screen. "What does it symbolise?"

"Faith," Sarah whispered. "And hope."

"Exactly. People's faith is brought alive at this time of year, and it's that which will bring them to the Nativity, just as long as we have something to put on for them." Gently turning her chin towards him, Harman smiled into her eyes. "You're an amazing person, Sarah, and I hope you realise that, no matter what happens."

Sarah gazed back at him, all else fading into the distance. Harman's smile deepened.

"And remember," he murmured, "'tis the season of miracles."

Sarah laughed to distract from her blushing, and grabbed her notebook.

"Then we can still do this. But we'll need favours – and lots of candles…"

It was Christmas Eve. St Saviour's pews were packed with bodies, some with hands wrapped round cups of mulled cider, others bundled up in coats and

a matter of days, the show went surprisingly well. Mary and Joseph reached Bethlehem safely, serenaded by *Little Donkey* and *Once in Royal David's City*. The innkeeper, played by real-life publican Dan Ferrers, was so effective in refusing them room that Mary, aka Chloe Denby, stopped waving at her parents and looked about to cry. Dan's hasty offer of the stable brought back her smile.

Angel Gabriel boomed out about the birth of the baby Jesus and with Jenny Lees leading the angel choir, *Away In A Manger* was sung.

Sarah cringed at the dance number that followed – lots of toe stamping and going the wrong way owing to so many original performers being absent. But

Mary, aka Chloe Denby, stopped waving at her parents and looked about to cry

scarves to keep out the chill as they awaited the start of the performance.

The candlelight added to the atmosphere as a group of white-clad, winged children came soft-footed down the aisle.

"Tonight," announced the organist's son, curls bouncing as he threw himself into his Angel Gabriel role, "will witness the greatest event since the world began."

His flock of angels dutifully aah'ed.

"For Mary and Joseph make their way to a town called Bethlehem…"

As Gabriel's beaming father played the first line of *O Little Town of Bethlehem*, Sarah sighed with relief. St Saviour's Nativity was underway.

It may not have been the masterpiece Linda originally planned but considering half the cast had only been rehearsing for

things moved swiftly on to shepherds and kings, all following the star drawn round the church by a leaping Gabriel. Then came the moment when Sarah could relax as Jenny Lees moved centre-stage.

A hush fell. Her white dress and gossamer wings made Jenny look ethereal. She opened her mouth and a sound, powerful in its purity, echoed around.

In the bleak midwinter, frosty wind made moan.

Sarah stared in wonder at this child, haloed in candlelight and holding the entire church in her palm. Closing her eyes, she let the heavenly voice wash over her. All the anxiety and last-minute alterations had been worth it, she thought, for this one magic moment when a star was born…

Continued overleaf

Festive

Continued from previous page

What shall I give him, poor as I am? The man stood in the doorway, no longer desperate. This place – and that voice – did strange things to him. He laid a newspaper article, folded at a certain image, in the donations basket.

The board outside cried that St Saviour's needed restoration funds. Well, what he'd hidden here should help raise the required readies. He doffed an imaginary cap to the statue in the alcove, then, smiling, slipped out into the twilight.

The carol finished. Jenny Lees bowed her head. The church erupted into rapturous applause and Sarah, laughing,

"Before your eyes?" she asked worriedly.

"In the crib," Chloe corrected, and plunging a hand into the straw, withdrew a pile of tiny, glittering diamonds.

Christmas morning felt more special than usual for the parish. After Rev Harman had linked Chloe's "stars" with the mysterious folded article he'd found, cataloguing items recently stolen from a Paris jeweller's, a few phone calls revealed the diamonds were part of a priceless antique necklace. Its return was set to earn St Saviour's a sizeable reward.

"Almost half the restoration fund," he told Sarah in an early-morning call.

"I mean, you probably have tons of better offers and you're really busy…"

clapped heartily with the rest. What a star!

As if inspired by little Miss Lees, the audience gave a ringing rendition of *Hark the Herald Angels Sing*, and cheered Rev Harman as he thanked them for coming.

Sarah hugged herself. Linda would be delighted by how well things had gone. She joined the group of parents gathered round the stage to add her congratulations to the performers, especially Jenny, then approached an oddly subdued Chloe Denby.

"What's wrong, darling?"

Chloe was staring at the crib in which she'd been rocking Baby Jesus.

"I'm seeing stars."

Sarah frowned. Not another 'flu victim!

"Your Christmas miracle. I'm so glad."

"Ours," he corrected. "I'm convinced it wouldn't have happened if it wasn't for you. You never gave up and staged an amazing show that brought out the goodwill in somebody. Er… I was wondering," he added, in much less than his normal, assured tone. "I mean, you probably have tons of better offers and you're really busy, but I'd love to take you to dinner one night. That is, if you…"

"I'd love that, too, Reverend," Sarah interrupted softly. "Now, hadn't you better go? You've got rather a busy day today."

"True, but there's one more thing. Do you think you could call me Richard?"

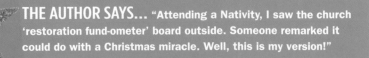

THE AUTHOR SAYS… "Attending a Nativity, I saw the church 'restoration fund-ometer' board outside. Someone remarked it could do with a Christmas miracle. Well, this is my version!"

BRAIN BOOSTERS SOLUTIONS

CODEBREAKER from Page 11

PHRASE: THERE MUST BE AN ANGEL (PLAYING WITH MY HEART)

KRISS KROSS from Page 63

MISSING LINK from Page 83
ACROSS: 1 Glass 4 Label 7 Firm 8 Accident 9 People 11 Bath 12 Bird 14 Grip 17 Tent 18 Orders 19 Dispatch 21 Beat 22 Medal 23 Right
DOWN: 1 Guinea 2 Arm 3 Stage 4 Locking 5 Bad 6 Length 10 Point 11 Blind 13 Digital 15 Medium 16 Breast 18 Other 20 Pad 21 Big
SHADED WORD: RETAIL

MISSING LINK from Page 115
ACROSS: 2 Nice 7 Queen 8 Practice 9 Rain 10 Personal 11 Knife 13 Warrant 14 Stool 17 District 19 Book 20 Designer 22 Paint 23 Flag
DOWN: 1 Top 2 National 3 Cocoa 4 Current 5 Relief 6 Fairy 10 Pass 11 Knitting 12 Exit 13 Working 15 Two-way 16 Giant 18 Ideal 21 Raw
SHADED WORD: TAXING

SUDOKU from Page 107

2	4	6	5	8	1	7	9	3
7	3	1	9	6	2	8	4	5
5	8	9	7	3	4	2	1	6
3	5	2	1	9	8	6	7	4
1	9	4	6	2	7	5	3	8
8	6	7	4	5	3	9	2	1
6	7	5	3	1	9	4	8	2
9	2	3	8	4	5	1	6	7
4	1	8	2	7	6	3	5	9

4	9	6	5	3	8	2	1	7
7	1	5	9	4	2	8	6	3
8	3	2	6	1	7	5	9	4
5	8	9	4	2	1	3	7	6
6	4	3	8	7	9	1	2	5
1	2	7	3	6	5	9	4	8
3	5	1	7	9	4	6	8	2
9	7	8	2	5	6	4	3	1
2	6	4	1	8	3	7	5	9

WORDWHEEL from Page 107
The nine-letter word is DEXTEROUS

Magic Man

Rest in peace, Grandad – full of fun and laughter. Even if you couldn't get my cousin and me to live in peace...

By Pat Holness

ur eyes meet for a fleeting second before we look away again.

Sadie is my cousin – or to put it more precisely, my estranged cousin. We fell out after a stupid quarrel years ago and the Cold War situation has remained in place ever since. We haven't even marked birthdays or exchanged Christmas cards since then,

I see from a sideways glance that today Sadie is looking immaculate in a black designer suit and elegant high heels. I have chosen a dove-grey dress with a black fitted jacket and comfy flats. Coping with sore feet is something I can do without at our beloved grandfather's funeral.

The organ is playing softly as we take our places in church, Sadie and I watching one another covertly like a couple of spies in case we choose seats too close for comfort.

It's all too ridiculous, of course, but as we sing the first hymn I cannot imagine how things are ever going to alter. We're set in our ways now, Sadie and I, both too old to embrace change – or one another, for that matter.

But today we're not here to rub salt in old wounds. We're here to celebrate the life of a kind, generous and loving old man. Our grandad.

As various members of his extended family step to the front of the church and recall incidents and memories from his life, I am lost in my own recollections.

He was a fun-loving man, our grandfather, born in the middle of the Second World War. He lived through times when money wasn't plentiful and luxury goods neither available nor affordable, so devotedly he taught his family to make their own entertainment on high days and holidays. Christmases spent in his rambling old house were always the best.

He showed us card games and got us chasing round his draughty rooms in the middle of winter, playing sardines. But best of all was when Grandad became Mr Monty the Magician.

His tricks were amazing to us as kids. He could make spoons vanish and small toys appear from beneath his famous white hanky, which featured in all the tricks.

Sometimes he would persuade Sadie and me to help him with his magic, but no matter how near to him we stood, we could never make out how he did the

Continued overleaf

Continued from previous page

tricks. It was the genuine thing as far as we were concerned.

Of course that was back in the days of childhood, before Sadie and I fell out.

"I wish you two would make it up," Grandad used to say, sometimes sadly. sometimes impatiently, once he'd got wind of our estrangement. "If only I could do one of my magic tricks and make you friends again, it would be marvellous."

But of course, that wasn't possible and Sadie and I took to visiting Grandad at different times, so that we wouldn't need to be in the same room together.

We remain in place for a few minutes, lost in our memories. A soft breeze blows caressingly and a watery winter sun emerges from the clouds as if to cast a blessing on the scene.

And then, suddenly, the wind snatches a white hanky from the hands of one of the mourners and wafts it across the

"If only I could do a magic trick and make you friends again..." he'd say

Now my mind is miles away when I realise the funeral service is over and Grandad's coffin is being borne out to the graveside.

A sideways glance reveals that like me, Sadie has tears in her eyes. Grandad loved us both so much, and now we're each going to feel the loss of this wonderful old man.

The saddest part of the funeral, the interment, is about to take place. Sadie and I stand on opposite sides of the grave while the vicar says his piece.

Few of the onlookers have dry eyes as we watch Grandad's coffin lowered reverently into the ground.

And then it's over.

graveside. It's just as if Grandad is performing one last magic trick as he leaves us behind.

I feel Sadie's eyes on me and look up to meet her gaze.

It's clear she's having exactly the same thought as I am.

And for the first time in many years, we smile at one another through our tears.

THE AUTHOR SAYS... "I was moved to write this story after thankfully witnessing a family making up their differences at a loved one's funeral."